EVALUATIVE
INQUIRY *for*
LEARNING *in*
ORGANIZATIONS

EVALUATIVE INQUIRY *for* LEARNING *in* ORGANIZATIONS

Hallie Preskill
Rosalie T. Torres

SAGE Publications
International Educational and Professional Publisher
Thousand Oaks   London   New Delhi

For information:

SAGE Publications, Inc.
2455 Teller Road
Thousand Oaks, California 91320
E-mail: order@sagepub.com

SAGE Publications Ltd.
6 Bonhill Street
London EC2A 4PU
United Kingdom

SAGE Publications India Pvt. Ltd.
M-32 Market
Greater Kailash I
New Delhi 110048 India

Printed in the United States of America

Library of Congress Cataloging-in-Publication Data

Preskill, Hallie S.
  Evaluative inquiry for learning in organizations / by Hallie
Preskill and Rosalie T. Torres.
    p. cm.
  Includes bibliographical references and index.
  ISBN 0-7619-0453-0 (acid-free paper)
  ISBN 0-7619-0454-9 (pbk. : acid-free paper)
  1. Organizational learning. 2. Inquiry (Theory of knowledge) I.
Torres, Rosalie T. II. Title.
  HD58.82 .P74 1998
  658.4'06—ddc21
                                                    98-40122

    00 01 02 03 04 05 8 7 6 5 4 3 2

Acquiring Editor:	*C. Deborah Laughton*
Editorial Assistant:	*Eileen Carr*
Production Editor:	*Denise Santoyo*
Designer/Typesetter:	*Danielle Dillahunt*
Cover Designer:	*Candice Harman*

Contents in Brief

Contents

List of Strategies, Exhibits, and Figures

Strategies

Exhibits

Figures

Acknowledgments

Writing a book such as this is not easily accomplished without the support and encouragement of many people. We first wish to thank those we interviewed in our field research. They gave generously of their time and provided us with critical insights into the relationship between organizational learning theory and practice. We have the greatest respect for them, as they represent the true agents of learning and change in organizations. We also wish to thank several of our colleagues who, over the last few years, gave us feedback on our ideas as they evolved. In particular, we would like to thank Michael Q. Patton, Brad Cousins, Valerie Caracelli, Larry Braskamp, Lyn Shulha, Jennifer Martineau, and our anonymous reviewers.

Once again, our editor, C. Deborah Laughton, gave unwavering support and guidance throughout the writing of this book. Her untiring good cheer, belief in the importance of this topic, and concrete suggestions made the writing process all the more enjoyable and worthwhile.

We have saved for last those individuals whose daily support meant being able to complete this book. To Stephen and Benjamin—your patience, sense of humor, and understanding during the last 2 years made writing this book possible.

Introduction

The amount of organizational change occurring today is unprecedented. The burgeoning literature that has provided advice, empirical research, case studies, and evaluations on this subject suggests that today's organizations (a) are context bound and driven, (b) are made of up people who experience change differently, (c) have many cultures, (d) include formal and informal communication structures, and (e) are politically charged.

Continuous organizational change is resulting in less organizational stability and a redefinition of who we are and what we do in the workplace. The traditional structures that have given us a feeling of solidity and predictability have vanished. This shift has placed a greater emphasis on the need for fluid processes that can change as an organization and its members' needs change. Instead of the traditional rational, linear, hierarchical approach to managing jobs, which focused on breaking down job tasks and isolating job functions, tomorrow's jobs will be built on establishing networks of relationships. Workers will require listening, communicating, and group facilitation skills to get their work done. As a result, more and more organizational charts, job descriptions, and functional specializations will go by the wayside.

Organizations that make it through this transition will provide "structures that promote the flow of ideas, build trust and a unity of purpose, tap the energy and creativity of the workforce, and translate ideas into new products, processes and services" (Goddard, 1990, p. 4).

The sum of these changes is that tomorrow's organizations will (a) accomplish their work through multidisciplinary teams; (b) have permeable boundaries; (c) be focused on mental tasks; (d) be participative, diverse, and innovative; (e) support a professional culture of commitment and results; and (f) value peer-to-peer relationships. Organizations that have these characteristics will develop the capacity for self-renewal through the interaction of their members and employ a systems thinking approach to how work is accomplished. Such organizations will develop a culture of continuous learning that influences the way the organization approaches its goals—whether they be increasing student achievement scores, improving the satisfaction of clients and customers, placing higher numbers of jobless people in decent-paying jobs, or improving the profit margin on a particular product.

As organizations adapt to new economic and societal requirements, we believe that evaluative inquiry can be a guiding force for organizational growth and success. When we (the authors) started working in the evaluation field some 20 years ago, program evaluation in the United States was still in its adolescence. Having been born in the early 1960s through federal grant requirements, evaluations typically were conducted by social science researchers employed in universities and government agencies. These evaluators were esteemed for their perceived unbiased, objective perspective. In most cases, they had been trained to use a strict social science positivist approach, emphasizing experimental designs and replicable, generalizable findings. They typically developed psychometrically valid instruments, collected data, conducted statistical analyses, and submitted a final report with recommendations to primary stakeholders.

The evaluation's role was to help reduce uncertainty by providing data and information for the purpose of decision making. It was assumed that organizations knew how to use such information and that they would do so, making the appropriate changes. Schwandt (1997) characterizes this mode of problem solving as an "operational intelligence" approach to evaluative activity:

> This kind of intelligence is instruction on the status of means and means-end reasoning; it is directed at helping a client get to there from here. . . . Evaluation aimed at teaching operational intelligence seeks to improve the rationality of practitioner and decision maker's practices by applying knowledge that evaluation has produced. (p. 79)

A rationalist approach to evaluation inquiry assumes that the organization is an independent actor in its environment, that there is only one answer to the question, that everyone thinks rationally on behalf of the organization and will arrive at the same conclusion, and that full implementation follows the discovery of the one best strategy. This approach has also focused on individual learning and short-term solutions rather than helping organizations learn about their practice and the values on which that practice is based.

Although this kind of thinking has served many organizations well over the years, it is inconsistent with the goal of developing a community of practitioners who inquire daily about their progress and use their learning to improve themselves and the organization. We are increasingly hearing from management experts that the key to organizational survival is, and will be, the intellectual capital of its employees. We're not talking just about business organizations—this relates to *every* kind of organization in every sector of society. Just as organizations need to transform themselves to survive, so must evaluation theory and practice evolve.

Thus, the question becomes: **How can evaluative inquiry contribute to the development, maintenance, and growth of organizations in a dynamic, unstable, unpredictable environment? What we propose in this book is that evaluative inquiry can not only be a means of accumulating information for decision making and action (operational intelligence) but that it also be equally concerned with questioning and debating the *value* of what we do in organizations.** This approach is much more aligned with the interpretive perspective of organizational learning. That is, learning from evaluative inquiry is a social construction occurring through the involvement of multiple constituencies each representing different perspectives. It is socially situated and is mediated through participants' previous knowledge and experiences.

We see evaluative inquiry as a kind of public philosophy in which organization members engage in dialogue with clients and other stakeholders about the meaning of what they do and how they do it. In this dialogue, they pay particular attention to the historical, political, and sociological aspects of the objects of inquiry (Schwandt, 1992). Evaluative inquiry for organizational learning and change encompasses

- A focus on program and organizational processes as well as outcomes
- Shared individual, team, and organizational learning
- Education and training of organizational practitioners in inquiry skills
- Modeling the behaviors of collaboration, cooperation, and participation
- Establishing linkages between learning and performance
- Searching for ways to create greater understanding of the variables that affect organizational success and failure
- Using a diversity of perspectives to develop understanding about organizational issues

The approach to evaluative inquiry we present in this book is a result of our cumulative experiences teaching evaluation, conducting research on evaluation practice, and providing consulting services to education, business, health care, government, and nonprofit organizations. Over the years, we have learned that in spite of an organization's interest in evaluation, the findings of our inquiry efforts, often reported in traditional lengthy final reports, have gone unused. The reports may have been read by some, but all in all, the changes called for in these documents were rarely implemented. Reasons for this situation included (a) the changes already had been implemented as program participants were monitoring their own progress, (b) the political climate had changed so that interest in the evaluation and its findings had diminished, or (c) a lack of initial buy-in to the evaluation limited the perceived usefulness of its findings. As we reflected on the reasons why our evaluation efforts failed to have the kinds of organizational impact we had hoped for, we came to realize that traditional evaluation practice is inadequate for helping today's organizations meet the complex challenges of a global economy and the emergence of the knowledge era. In addition, evaluation, as we and many others have been practicing it, has not paid attention to the learning dimensions of evaluative activity. We first addressed this problem with Mary Piontek in our book on evaluation strategies for communicating and reporting (Torres, Preskill, & Piontek, 1996; also see Torres, Preskill, & Piontek, 1997). This new book represents a more comprehensive reconceptualization of evaluation practice as a set of processes that leads to individual, team, and organizational learning.

Our goals for writing this book are to

- Describe the role of evaluative inquiry in learning organizations
- Provide a framework for conducting evaluative inquiry within an organizational learning context
- Stimulate reflection and conversation among evaluators, researchers, organizational members, and consultants about their own practice

This book offers readers a way of thinking about and conducting evaluative inquiry in every kind of organization. We believe that by integrating evaluative inquiry into an organization's work processes, organization members will be better able to meet the demands of tomorrow's challenges.

FOR WHOM DID WE WRITE THIS BOOK?

This book was written for evaluators, managers, administrators, researchers, consultants, trainers, staff development and organization development practitioners, and leaders in education, health care, business and industry, government, and nonprofit organizations. It is for those individuals who wish to use evaluative inquiry as a catalyst for organizational change, growth, and renewal. It is for those who believe learning is a lifelong process that is never finished. Finally, it is for people who believe in developing communities of practice where work is best accomplished through interpersonal relationships and dialogue.

It is important to recognize that this book addresses both theoretical and practical issues associated with conducting evaluative inquiry. It is an attempt to bridge what research says about individual, team, and organizational learning *and* evaluation. This book is neither a primer on organizational learning nor a textbook on evaluation. For both of these topics, there are many excellent resources.[1] Instead, this book tries to answer the questions "How does evaluative inquiry contribute to organizational learning?" and "How do we practice evaluative inquiry in ways that maximize individual and team learning?" We hope this book provides readers with another way to conceptualize both (a) organizational learning and change and (b) evaluation.

We've chosen to focus on using evaluative inquiry processes within organizations—versus across large-scale, multisite programs or within a public policy arena. The processes described in the book build on local and working knowledge and therefore are most readily applied within a specific organizational context. At the same time, we hope that those working in policy-making environments will also find the ideas and strategies discussed in the book useful.

OUR FIELD RESEARCH

The ideas expressed in this book represent our collective experience, our reading of the extant literature, and in-depth interviews we conducted in organizations that were attempting to implement organizational learning practices. These include

- Land O' Lakes (Minneapolis, MN)
- Colorado Department of Education—The Prevention Initiatives Unit (Denver, CO)
- Ford Motor Company—Electrical, Fuel, and Handling Division (Ypsilanti, MI)

- Presbyterian Hospital and Healthcare Services (Albuquerque, NM)

Specifically, we were interested in knowing (a) how the organization became interested in organizational learning principles and practices; (b) the nature of organizational support needed for implementing organizational learning practices; (c) what specific strategies were being used to facilitate and support individual, team, and organizational learning; and (d) what the organization perceived to be concrete outcomes of implementing organizational learning practices. We also asked our interviewees to explain if, and how, they were evaluating any of these efforts.

During our 1- to 3-day site visits, we interviewed a total of 28 individuals. Throughout the book, we have integrated quotations from our interviewees and from others we have met over the last 2 years with whom we've discussed our ideas. Each of the quotations used is referenced by the person's initials and organization, and by the location of the quotation in our data file. In addition, all quotations were approved for use in this book by the interviewees.

OVERVIEW OF THE BOOK

The first three chapters of this book lay the foundation and context for evaluative inquiry. In Chapter 1, we discuss how organizations are changing and the necessary conditions for organizational survival in the 21st century. We make the case that organizations will need to develop communities of inquirers that capitalize on the knowledge and expertise of those closest to organizational issues, and that evaluative inquiry can be the driving force for this effort.

In Chapter 2, we define and discuss what it means to learn at the individual, team, and organizational levels. If organizations are to benefit from evaluative inquiry, it is important to understand how learning occurs at each of these levels. Chapter 3 describes the four learning processes that facilitate evaluative inquiry. These are dialogue, reflection, asking questions, and identifying and clarifying values, beliefs, assumptions, and knowledge. Engaging these processes throughout evaluative inquiry efforts will develop greater insights and understandings about organizational issues. Ultimately, these insights and understandings lead to informed decisions necessary for organizational change.

The next three chapters guide the reader through the three phases of evaluative inquiry. In Chapter 4, we explain how an evaluative inquiry team goes about focusing the inquiry using the four learning processes. The steps described in this chapter include defining the issue, identifying stakeholders, and determining evaluative questions the inquiry will address. In Chapter 5, we describe how to carry out the inquiry, again using the four learning processes to facilitate the tasks of this phase. In this chapter, we cover issues related to the inquiry's design, data collection, analysis and interpretation, recommendations, and communicating and reporting. Chapter 6 focuses on applying learning from the evaluative inquiry. It covers identifying and selecting action alternatives, developing action plans, and implementing and monitoring the actions taken. Through each of these three chapters, we have interwoven an illustrative case to help the reader clearly understand how the four learning processes are used during each of the evaluative inquiry phases. Additionally, Chapters 4, 5, and 6 include specific strategies (in boxed text) for implementing evaluative inquiry.

In Chapter 7, we argue that for evaluative inquiry to be successful, an organization's infrastructure must support and facilitate it. The critical elements of this infrastructure are culture, leadership, communication, and systems and structures. How each of these relates to evaluative inquiry is discussed in detail with examples provided from our research. Chapter 8 addresses additional considerations for the practice of evaluative inquiry. It compares evaluative inquiry for organizational learning and change to more traditional approaches to evaluation and organization development. In addition, it explores evaluator roles and challenges to implementing evaluative inquiry in today's organizations.

The reader can take any of several routes in reading this book. For the fullest understanding of what constitutes evaluative inquiry and why it is an important approach to understanding organizational life, it is best to start with Chapter 1 and read the chapters in sequence. Readers already familiar with the literature on organizational change and theories of individual, team, and organizational learning may wish to begin with Chapter 3, which describes the four learning processes central to evaluative inquiry. They would then read Chapters 4 through 6, the "how to conduct evaluative inquiry" chapters. After acquiring a thorough understanding of what evaluative inquiry entails, the reader should then read Chapter 7, which addresses what needs to be present in the larger organization infrastructure for successful implementation of evaluative inquiry. Regardless of the road taken, we hope readers will develop an understanding of how evaluative inquiry can be a catalyst for learning in organizations. Although the journey no doubt will be a difficult one, the challenges experienced along the way may reveal unanticipated hidden treasures.

NOTE

1. For example, see the following books, which provide an overview of the theory and practice of evaluation: Herman (1987), Joint Committee on Standards for Educational Evaluation (1994), Patton (1997), Posavac and Carey (1997), Shadish, Cook, and Leviton (1991), and Worthen, Sanders, and Fitzpatrick (1997).

Books on the theory and practice of organizational learning include Argyris (1992), Argyris and Schon (1996), Chawla and Renesch (1995), Cohen and Sproull (1996), DiBella and Nevis (1998), Dixon (1994), Marquardt (1996a), and Watkins and Marsick (1993).

CHAPTER 1

Evaluative Inquiry and Organizational Change

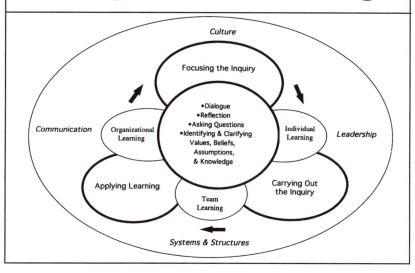

We envision evaluative inquiry as an ongoing process for inves-
tigating and understanding critical organizational issues. It
is an approach to learning that is fully integrated with an
organization's work practices, and as such, it engenders (a) organization
members' interest and ability in exploring critical issues using evalu-

ation logic, (b) organization members' involvement in evaluative processes, and (c) the personal and professional growth of individuals within the organization.

Evaluative inquiry represents an emphasis on understanding each other in order to understand larger organizational challenges. Consequently, inquiry becomes a social and communal activity in which critical organizational issues are constructed by a varied and broadly based community of inquirers. These issues are subjected to continuous reconsideration and reexamination through a dialogic process involving many diverse participants. In essence, evaluative inquiry is about practical wisdom and organization members deliberating about what is good and expedient, with an emphasis on using data to inform learning and action. In this chapter, we define evaluative inquiry and describe its role within changing organizations and the needs of tomorrow's workplaces.

Evaluative inquiry is particularly important for today's organizations because employees are being required to do more and more with fewer and fewer resources. They are increasingly being asked to make quick decisions and find they have little quality data on which to make those decisions. As the need to change accelerates, the cost of making uninformed decisions will be terribly high, possibly resulting in the failure of critical human service and education programs and whole industries. Evaluative inquiry offers organizations a process for collaborating on issues that challenge success. Through the collective action of dialogue, reflection, asking questions, and identifying and clarifying individuals' values, beliefs, assumptions, and knowledge, evaluative inquiry provides organization members with an approach to inquiry that results in learning about significant organizational issues.

Fundamental to organization members' ability to implement evaluative inquiry is an infrastructure that supports a learning culture, leadership that values learning, communication systems that facilitate frequent and easy access to information, and integrated systems and structures that characterize how work is accomplished (see Chapter 7). Inquiry becomes the catalyst not only for continuous growth and improvement toward meeting the organization's goals but also for the organization's employees—those individuals who make up the lifeblood of all organizations.

Carolyn Thompson, Director of Organizational Learning at Presbyterian Healthcare Services in Albuquerque, New Mexico, describes the importance of inquiry in her professional practice:

> I personally have come to realize that the questions are so much more important than the answers right now, especially in times of chaos. Inquiry of course is not something that you learn overnight. "Okay. We learned inquiry." The practice of inquiry is what deepens meaning, understanding, and the curiosity. (CT, Pres: 208)[1]

At its very heart, evaluative inquiry helps organization members reduce uncertainty, clarify direction, build community, and ensure that learning is part of everyone's job.

In the remainder of this chapter, we discuss the circumstances facing organizations that make their pursuit of evaluative inquiry ever more essential for their well-being and survival. These circumstances include (a) the nature of change organizations are currently experiencing, (b) the transition from the industrial to the knowledge era, (c) the failure of past change efforts, and (d) the role of learning in our future.

ORGANIZATIONAL CHANGE AS THE STATUS QUO

Organizations are in a constant state of change. In only a few years, this statement has become a cliché. What has become crystal clear is that organizations will never again be stable and predictable entities. No longer do organizations offer one product or service for 20 or more years with a homogeneous workforce that experiences little turnover. Peter Vaill (1996) has captured the spirit of these unprecedented organizational changes as "permanent white water." For organizations immersed in white water, (a) life will be full of surprises; (b) increasing complexity will produce novel problems; (c) events will be messy, ambiguous, and ill-structured; (d) events often will be quite costly; and

(e) the recurrence of problem issues will be a significant continuing challenge.

It is generally believed that three forces are working to create these changes. They are globalization, workforce demographics, and technology (Drucker, 1997; Judy & D'Amico, 1997; McLagan & Nel, 1996). Never before has the world seemed so small. With decreasing communication and transportation costs, the volume of goods and services traded across national boundaries has expanded. "Financial markets already electronically move one trillion dollars a day, crossing borders as they please" (Mandl & Sethi, 1996, p. 259). No longer are people, organizations, or nations isolated. With increasing uses of fax machines, phones, and computers, companies now design, manufacture, and sell their services and products in several different countries. The role of foreign trade in the American economy is between two and three times as important as it was in 1965 (Judy & D'Amico, 1997). Employees are now free to work outside the geographical boundaries of their company; they can be anywhere in the world. For example, the globalization of information technology means that "programmers in India and other foreign nations will provide software and other engineering services to American customers" (Judy & D'Amico, 1997, p. 20). As developing and historically communist and socialist countries increase their ability to import and export goods and services, and develop a coterie of knowledge workers, competition will continue to stimulate ongoing organizational change in all sectors of the world's economy.

A second driving force of organizational change is the transformation of the workforce. Drucker (1997) compares today's changing workforce to the introduction of agriculture or the Industrial Revolution in terms of its impact. He cites the emigration of peoples from Asia, Southeast Asia, the Pacific Islands, Central and South America, the Caribbean, and West and East Africa as having significant effects on the future of the U.S. workforce.

> Numerous racial and ethnic groups; differing languages, communication patterns, and cultural values; an altered workplace structure and dynamics; and new patterns of educational and training

demands are becoming commonplace and go well beyond the scope of traditional corporate cultures. (Drucker, 1997, p. 77)

Within just a few years, it is estimated that 30-40% of all new entrants into the labor force will be those from nonwhite cultural and ethnic groups (Drucker, 1997; Loveman & Gabarro, 1991). In the European Community, it is estimated that between 1990 and 2040, the working population will fall by 20% while the aging population will increase dramatically (Johnson, 1996). Aging baby boomers are also affecting the U.S. economy. With the average life span increasing every year due to better health care, diets, and lifestyles, there is an increasing demand for the goods and services required or desired by those in their later years (Judy & D'Amico, 1997).

Technology is the third major force affecting significant organizational change. Several writers suggest that information technology will revolutionize the world's production and consumption capacities and needs, as well as the way work is accomplished (Drucker, 1997; Judy & D'Amico, 1997; March, 1995; McKenney, Copeland, & Mason, 1995; Tapscott, 1995, Zuboff, 1988). The increasing reliance on technology in all aspects of work life (not to mention personal life) requires that people change how they make things, provide services, and communicate with one another.

In the early years of technology, computers were used primarily to maintain, process, and analyze data. For example, in schools, computers often were used mainly for drill and practice exercises, rewarding students, or tracking student progress. Today, however, computer technology is changing the way we develop processes, services, products, and learning. It is influencing the shift from a decentralization and control of operational processes into holistic, integrated systems. As networked technology is used by different people in different locations around the world, it undercuts the traditional hierarchical management systems, thus "redirecting the flow of information . . . unrestrained by the tether of time, distance, and departmental persuasion" (Mandl & Sethi, 1996, p. 261).

Technology is also facilitating learning through the use of help screens, on-line tutorials, database searches, computer conferences, electronic bulletin boards, electronic mail, performance support systems, and electronic dialogues. These informal learning tools enable users to obtain information when they need it and provide real-time communications regardless of geographic location. Space and time have become invisible to learning.

Evidence of the increasing use of technology for training is reported in the 1997 industry report published by *Training Magazine* (Training Magazine Industry Report, 1997). The survey of a stratified random sample of subscribers revealed the following:

- 94% of the organizations (with more than 100 employees) provide basic computer skills to their employees
- 29% of all formal training provided pertains to computers and computer systems
- 24% of technical training was delivered through technological means (up from 17% in 1996)
- 66% of the respondents say their departments use an on-line service regularly for research or information gathering purposes, and 55% use it for e-mail and other forms of communication; 22% say their organizations recruit new employees on-line
- 12% of the organizations use electronic performance support systems (up from 5% in 1996)
- 54% are using teleconferencing for business meetings, and 35% of the organizations are using technology for distance learning

Communication and information technologies are expected to provide organizations with many benefits. First, information can be disseminated in a timely way to employees, clients, suppliers, and customers. Second, work can be performed from a distance, allowing greater linkages with both internal and external clients. Third, employees working from home will allow organizations to reduce overhead costs and increase employees' control over how they structure their work time. Fourth, instructional television, distance education, computer-based training, and video technologies can be used to educate and cross-train employees across sites. Ultimately, these uses of technology will fundamentally change how we perceive the boundaries of work (Goodman, Sproull, & Associates, 1990; Mandl & Sethi, 1996). (In Chapter 7, we discuss more about technology, communication, and an organization's infrastructure.)

TRANSITIONING TO THE KNOWLEDGE ERA

Increased globalization, changing workforce demographics, and technology are all related to the emergence of the knowledge era, in which knowledge, not physical labor, has become the "key raw material for wealth creation and is the fountain of organizational and personal power" (Marquardt & Reynolds, 1994, p. 9). Knowledge, or intellectual capital, is fast becoming the essential organizational asset as compared to the importance of buildings, material resources, markets, and goods and services in former times (Allee, 1997; March, 1995; Morris, 1995; Stewart, 1997). Intellectual capital is the collective brainpower of organization members—it is knowledge, information, intellectual property, and experience (Stewart, 1997). Organizations that make the transition to the knowledge era will learn how to generate, use, and sell information, regardless of the business they are in. (Davis, 1996). Exhibit 1.1 highlights some of the major changes required of organizations as they enter the 21st century. As one can see, the changes from the industrial era to the knowledge era represent fundamentally different ways of viewing the relationship between workers and management. The knowledge era will emphasize cooperation, collaboration, autonomy, being proactive, long-term thinking, and learning.

Drucker (1997), however, is particularly concerned about the world's demographics in this new era. For him, the problem is not overpopulation but underpopulation of the developed countries that have been providing knowledge workers. Drucker (1997) argues that knowledge is different from other kinds of resources. "It constantly makes itself obsolete, with the result that today's advanced knowledge is tomorrow's ignorance" (p. 22). He warns that the productivity of knowledge and

EXHIBIT 1.1.

Transitioning From the
Industrial Era to the Knowledge Era

Industrial Era	Knowledge Era
Hierarchical chain of command	Self-governing teams and networks
Competitive advantage	Collaborative advantage
Control	Commitment
Managers control, maintain stability	Managers coach and lead
Few performance information systems	Proliferation of performance information systems
Multiple levels of management	Fewer layers of management
Bureaucratic rules and policies	Fewer rules and policies
Power over others	Sharing power with others
Information held by a few	Information disseminated and available to all
Emphasis on repetition	Emphasis on problem solving
Risk averse	Risk tolerant
Interest in short-term gains	Interest in continuous improvement and long-term gains

knowledge workers will be the decisive factor for success in most industries in developed countries. (See Chapter 7 for more on knowledge workers as part of an organization's infrastructure.)

Some futurists predict that as information created doubles every 3 to 4 years, the development and dissemination of knowledge are what will separate successful from less successful organizations in the coming years. The need for shared information and collaboration among organization members is a significant theme in the management literature. As Wheatley (1994) suggests, we need a broad distribution of information, viewpoints, and interpretations if we are to make sense of the world" (p. 64). The importance of information gathering has been discussed by several authors. They suggest that organizations that wish to learn and grow

- Are hungry for information and strive to communicate that knowledge with organization members who may benefit from it (Wick & Leon, 1993)
- Acquire "new information and the ability to analyze that information creatively, learn from it, and apply that learning in useful ways" (Thompson, 1995, p. 95)
- Provide "information regarding the bigger picture—information relevant to how the various parts fit together" (Mohrman, Cohen, & Mohrman, 1995, p. 182)

Zuboff (1988) believes that "becoming an information economy means driving a stake through the heart of the old division of labor," and that learning has become the new form of labor (p. 7). The future of organizations will also depend on their ability to transfer knowledge from one part of the organization to another, learn more effectively from their mistakes, and stimulate continuous improvement throughout the organization. Some evidence of this shift to focusing on learning can be seen in the job titles of those responsible for facilitating employees' learning and performance. Instead of traditional titles such as Training Director or Human Resource Development Manager, titles such as Director of Intellectual Capital, Chief Learning Officer, Chief Knowledge Officer, Knowledge Champion, and Director of Intellectual Asset Management are cropping up in all kinds of organizations (Allee, 1997; Galagan & Wulf, 1996; Willis & May, 1997). Results from a survey conducted with human resource development executives from *Fortune* 500 companies (American Society for Training and Development [ASTD], 1997) show that many organizations are becoming familiar with the notion of intellectual capital, though nearly half have only heard of it within the last year. Whether or not respondents had heard of "intellectual capital," 90% believe it is an important issue. At the same time, 59% think it might possibly be another buzzword or fad. Not everyone, however, believes that intellectual capital is just another management guru's hottest idea. Certainly, those sponsoring the Second World Congress on the Management of Intellectual Capital held at McMaster University in Canada (January, 1998) did not think so. In their invitation to participate in the conference they wrote:

> In the last century, Karl Marx claimed that owners of capital possessed society's true wealth. Today, as we turn into the 21st century, it is brainpower and information which are fast becoming the essential assets of society and the competitive weapons of choice.
>
> Intellectual Capital includes the intangible assets of skills, knowledge and information. Managing intellectual capital demands the encouragement of innovation, motivation of personnel, exploitation of patents and the building of knowledge-based companies without substantial traditional assets. (Bart, 1998)

To harness the intellectual capital of organizations requires an ability to adapt with speed and flexibility, to learn, and to remain open to change and new possibilities (Ashkenas, Ulrich, Jick, & Kerr, 1995; Hastings, 1996; Mink, Mink, Downes, & Owen, 1994). Functional and hierarchical organizational structures are too cumbersome and rigid to respond to a "constantly changing kaleidoscope of relationships between people" (Hastings, 1996, p. 7). In an attempt to be more responsive and flexible to these changes, organizations have reconceptualized and reconfigured themselves into virtual organizations, network organizations, boundaryless organizations, web organizations, and empowered organizations (Ashkenas et al., 1995). Characteristics of these newly configured organizations are (a) radical decentralization, (b) intense interdependence, (c) higher expectations, (d) transparent performance standards, (e) distributed leadership, (f) boundary busting, and (g) networking and reciprocity (Hastings, 1996, p. 7).

For many organizations, however, the requirement to change is happening too fast. A survey of 400 business executives from Fortune 1000 companies, conducted by the Gallup Organization (B. F., 1994), found that executives are ill-equipped to manage the changes they face. Fifty-six percent report they have no formal structure in place to handle change. When asked how their companies manage change, the study's authors found many contradictions:

> Almost all the executives (98%) rated their companies' ability to plan, control or adapt to change as capable or very capable, but only a slim majority (53%) actually anticipate the need to change and act in advance. The remaining 47% either handle change as it comes along or struggle to keep up. (p. 136)

It also appears that organizational leaders are not being prepared to deal with such massive organizational changes. As reported in the National Human Resource Development Executives Survey (ASTD, 1996c), only 22% of the respondents indicated that their company provides training on "managing change," and only 12% said they offer training on "strategic planning." Whether leaders and organizations are prepared or not, change has become a way of organizational life—something that happens daily, not every 5 to 10 years.

FAILURE OF PAST CHANGE EFFORTS

As organizations have responded to the needs of changing societies and economies, they have made numerous efforts to restructure, reengineer, and reform themselves into what futurists and management theorists have recommended. Continuous Quality Improvement (CQI) and Total Quality Management (TQM) were developed in response to problems with processes and procedures within organizations. These programs provided a means for employees to analyze underlying causes and tweak processes so that they would work better. For the most part, these efforts resulted in cause-effect kinds of actions that left processes prone to breaking again. Reengineering, on the other hand, asked that organization members think more systemically about problems they were experiencing. The assumption guiding these initiatives was that the organization needed new processes, new jobs, and new employees with different approaches to solving problems and accomplishing goals.

In spite of the billions of dollars that have been spent in the name of these and other change initiatives, most organizations have failed to achieve the desired results. They have failed because organization members have not been provided with the necessary environment and opportunities to learn from their own and others' experiences in implementing new forms of practice (Garvin, 1993; McGill & Slocum, 1993; Preskill, 1994; Senge, 1990a; Watkins & Marsick, 1993).

Hord (1997) writes that the quick-fix mentality, particularly prevalent in the United States, has resulted in schools making changes that have been poorly planned and implemented. She calls this approach to educational reform the "microwave oven" theory, whereby educational institutions "pop a new program in for four minutes with a hero principal managing it and improvement is done" (p. v). This approach rarely leads to real sustainable changes in schools. Accompanying this quick-fix mentality is the fact that, in most cases, the strategies schools have implemented in the name of educational reform have not focused on things that matter or that make a difference (Fullan, 1993). As Fullan admonishes, *"to restructure, is not to reculture"* (p. 49).

In many respects, many change efforts have fallen short because organizational leaders have failed to acknowledge the complex nature of organizational life. As a result, organizations have experienced (a) poorly implemented change strategies; (b) an inability of merged companies to integrate employees; (c) costly delays in delivering products and services, and in initiating changes; (d) little increase in productivity from downsizing; and (e) the lack of significant financial results from quality improvement programs (Kotter, 1996). In the end, however, change efforts such as CQI, TQM, and reengineering have failed because organizations have not factored in the organization's culture, the ways in which employees change, and how people learn. Ultimately, the results of downsizing, discontinuing products and services, and eliminating divisions have contributed to a loss of employee loyalty, commitment, and trust in many organizations.

One reason organizations have latched on to the "microwave theory" is because managers and leaders have not been acculturated to seek a more comprehensive understanding of causes, to experiment with strategies, or to foresee problems; instead, they have been trained to react to issues in shortsighted ways. The piecemeal approach to "fixing" problems has led to linear, stopgap approaches to addressing organizational issues (McGill & Slocum, 1993). Making matters worse, few organizations have conducted any evaluations of these efforts to understand why, where, and how these efforts may have failed. For example, none of the organizations we visited had made any attempts to evaluate the implementation, impact, or effectiveness of their organizational learning practices and processes. One organization in particular was concerned that its efforts might be curtailed because it could not "prove" that what it was doing in the name of "organizational learning" made a difference. Many believed, however, that increased profits were due to specific organizational learning efforts.

THE ROLE OF LEARNING IN OUR FUTURE

For many organizations, a positive outcome from experimentation with various quality and improvement strategies has been a realization that the most effective way to meet their goals in this fluid, technological, knowledge-based, global environment is to reconsider the ways in which employees work and learn in organizations. Chalofsky (1996) believes that organizations need to shift from

- learning based on minimal competence to learning based on *continual improvement.*
- learning based on fear of failure to learning based on *risk taking.*
- learning based on individual performance to learning based on *team and collective performance.*

- learning based on competition to learning based on *cooperation and collaboration.*
- learning based on appraisal and criticism to learning based on *coaching, support, and feedback.*
- learning that is formal to learning that is *informal.*
- learning based on one right answer to learning based on *discovery of possibilities.*
- learning based on abstract, logical reasoning to learning based on *intuition, relationships, and context.*
- learning based on outcome (the destination) to learning based on *process* (the journey) (p. 292).

This paradigm acknowledges that learning is intentional and contextual, and it involves developing systems and structures that not only allow but also encourage organization members to learn and grow together—to develop "communities of practice."

Palmer (1987) defines community as "a capacity for relatedness within individuals—relatedness not only to people but to events in history, to nature, to the world of ideas, and yes, to things of the spirit" (p. 24). He believes that the "act of knowing itself is a way of building and rebuilding community" (p. 24). Spear (1993) suggests that learning community members are connected not only by work tasks but also by "matters of heart as well as the mind" (p. 11). Peck (1987) defines a learning community as "A group of individuals who have learned to communicate honestly with each other, whose relationships go deeper than their masks of composure . . . and who delight in each other, make others' conditions our own" (p. 59). As we can see in Exhibit 1.2, a learning community emphasizes learning through interactions with others in a respectful, humanizing, civil way.

At an implementation level, communities of practice are informal, continuous, and naturally occurring in organizations. Lave and Wenger first coined the term "communities of practice" in their 1991 book *Situated Learning.* They talk about practice as a social construction and suggest that practice includes both the explicit and implicit. Wenger (1997) writes that "learning is the engine of practice, and practice is the

EXHIBIT 1.2.

Characteristics of Learning Communities

Organization members:

▲ *Pursue issues of common interest and practice*
▲ *Seek consensus in decision-making processes*
▲ *Are empowered to act*
▲ *Rely on one another for information and learning*
▲ *See themselves as part of a larger whole—more than the sum of their individual relationships*
▲ *Support the sharing of divergent ideas*
▲ *Respect each other's gifts*
▲ *Engage in self-examination*
▲ *Engage in critical reflection*
▲ *Provide opportunities to hear dissenting opinions*
▲ *Create a spirit of cooperation, not competition*

history of that learning. As a consequence, communities of practice have life cycles that reflect such a process" (p. 39). Learning communities exist within organizations that ascribe to a philosophy of democratic accountability, a reconception of the role of the individual in organizations, and an acceptance that change starts at the individual level, with individuals taking responsibility for the collective outcomes of their own and the organization's practices. Employees who come together in this way possess a

> shared sense of what has to happen to get the job done. They develop a common way of thinking and talking about their work. . . . It is these groups where some of the most valuable and most innovative work-related learning occurs (Stamps, 1997, p. 36).

Learning communities or communities of practice are designed so that employees are empowered to act. Kemmis (quoted in Schratz, 1993) writes that learning communities must be

> able to reflect openly on the consequences of their actions. By subjecting our experience to joint self-reflection, we may incorporate wider group understandings and create a shared language and a shared identity—an identity formed in cooperative action and cooperative self-reflection. (p. 61)

When we consider that modern organizations have been organized primarily around employee specialties, fragmented processes, and discrete organizational functions, it is not surprising that changing to a more holistic, systemic approach to work is being perceived as a "Galilean Shift" by organization theorists (Kofman & Senge, 1993). Learning communities, however, help organization members see how the connections between fragmented thinking and acting limit community building (Spear, 1993). As organizations continue to experience rapid and significant changes, and increasingly recognize and value the intellectual capital of their members, learning communities may be thought of as a means to achieve organizational success.

Evaluative inquiry can contribute to the development of learning communities by providing organization members with a vocabulary and set of processes with which to address important organizational issues. Because evaluative inquiry depends on an understanding of how individuals, teams, and organizations learn, we provide the reader with a brief overview of key learning theories and concepts for each of these topics in Chapter 2.

NOTE

1. Source notes for quotations in this format refer to the interviewee, the interviewee's organization, and location in the authors' data files.

CHAPTER 2

Learning in Organizations

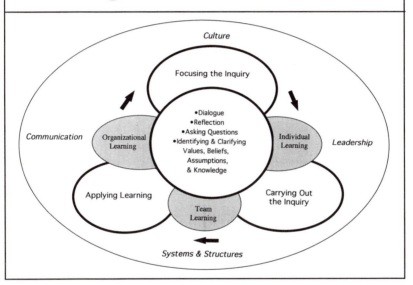

E valuative inquiry is a means for fostering individual and team learning about complex organizational issues. Evaluative inquiry for organizational learning and change is more than a means to an end; it is more than developing skills that result in increased competence or improved profits. A significant consequence of evaluative inquiry is the fostering of relationships among organization members and the diffusion of their learning throughout the organization; it serves as a transfer-of-knowledge process. To that end, evaluative inquiry provides an avenue for individuals' as well as the organization's ongoing growth and development.

In this chapter, we describe what it means to learn at the individual, team, and organizational levels, and how these levels of learning are related to evaluative inquiry. The reader may notice that we devote a significant amount of space to various aspects of developing and implementing a team-based approach to evaluative inquiry. For example, we address issues such as setting ground rules for team meetings, developing effective team processes, dealing with conflict among team members, and challenges to effective teamwork. We have chosen to emphasize the use of teams in implementing evaluative inquiry activities because teams are, in many ways, a microcosm of the larger organization. Teams provide the means for supporting individual as well as organizational learning. Although we believe that a team-based approach to evaluative inquiry maximizes the quality of the process and its findings, we also acknowledge that successful teamwork is not a simple undertaking; many issues need to be considered for teams to function successfully. Before we address team and organizational learning, however, we first explore what it means to learn from evaluative inquiry at the individual level.

HOW INDIVIDUALS LEARN

Over the years, several theories of adult learning have been explored and discussed. In this section, we provide a brief overview of some of these theories and describe how they may influence the ways in which individuals learn from evaluative inquiry.

Early definitions of learning suggested that learning is a change in behavior. Based on *behaviorism*, this definition views learning as an end product that focuses on the permanency of a desired change. Behaviorists such as Thorndike, Pavlov, Watson, and Skinner believed that as learners respond to stimuli in the environment, anticipated changes in behavior are produced. The role of the teacher, according to behaviorism, is to provide the environment and opportunity to elicit the desired response. Educational efforts such as the development of behavioral objectives, competency-based instruction, and skill development in training are examples of this orientation (Merriam & Caffarella, 1991).

Cognitive learning theories suggest that cognitive processes control learning and behavior; learning is mostly involuntary, and learners react mechanistically to feedback. Cognitive theories focus on how learning occurs, but explain little about why people learn. Contrary to behaviorist and cognitive learning theories, which typically view learners as passive participants in the learning process, *constructivist* learning theories suggest that learning is about "making meaning." Mezirow (1991) positions this type of learning within the communicative domain where most significant learning occurs. As Percival (1996) explains:

> Communicative learning enables us to understand and be understood; we learn to interact symbolically on the basis of meaning structures that have been shaped by culture, language, norms, and expectations. (p. 137)

This view asserts that adults learn when they assimilate new experiences and create new knowledge structures (Kolb, 1984). This reconstruction or transformation of knowledge affects subsequent thinking and performance. Constructivism is concerned with how people process information in ways that affect their worldview. It proposes that individuals continually create and re-create meaning as a result of their relationship with others in the social environment. *Constructivism* is particularly well suited for understanding interpersonal relationships and how behavior is mediated by organizational environments. Constructivist learning theories are built on the belief that all knowledge is based on experience and that meanings are arrived at by continually seeking order in these experiences. In this sense, we are not passive learners, as behaviorists would argue, but active learners, always growing and changing as a result of our social interactions (Jackson & MacIssac, 1994).

Adding the sociocultural variable to learning, *social constructivism* theory views learners as active agents in the construction of outcomes and stresses that the social setting itself is an evolving construction. When members of a social setting (e.g., an organization) share their social constructs, the cycle of learning is renewed. The teacher who operates from a perspective of social constructivist theory acts as a model and guide throughout the learning process.

Drawing on Dewey's (1938) claim that learning is a continuous process of the reconstruction of experience, others suggest that learning occurs when individuals have a "shared concrete experience;" they share their reactions and observations from the experience, generalize the experience to other aspects of life, and apply the learning to new situations (Jarvis, 1992; Kolb, 1984). Friere (1970) has noted the importance of "experiential realities" and has recommended that groups answer their own questions by raising the "critical consciousness" of the group. Action and reflection (often through an ongoing dialectic), however, must be included in the learning process to ensure that individuals learn from experience rather than just have experience (Watkins & Marsick, 1993).

Humanist learning theories, most commonly associated with Maslow and Rogers, also suggest that learning is guided by the learner's self-identified needs and past experiences. These theories emphasize that learners do best when there is a focus on problem-solving (Friere, 1970; Rogers, 1969), and when learners are responsible for identifying, designing, and evaluating their own learning objectives (Knowles, 1980; Merriam & Caffarella, 1991; Tough, 1979).

The practice of evaluative inquiry draws on each of these adult learning theories. For example, individuals might achieve a higher level of data collection and analysis competence when they use inquiry skills and receive feedback about how well they are doing (behaviorism). From their engagement in evaluative inquiry, individuals might come to understand an issue more fully and thus have a new appreciation of the issue (constructivism). They also may have developed an increased ability to think about the evaluative concern differently by employing new cognitive cues (cognitive learning). By collaboratively addressing the evaluative issue, and by identifying evaluative questions that are most relevant to their practice (social constructivism), individuals may learn from each other through evaluative inquiry. Finally, as individuals work on addressing a problem or issue through evaluative inquiry, they draw on their own needs and experiences (humanism), thereby increasing the depth of their learning.

In addition to understanding how adults generally learn, we also know that individuals have preferences for how they learn. These preferences are often referred to as *learning styles* and are associated with the choices people make during the learning process. Such choices typically affect how information is selected and processed (Harris & DeSimone, 1994). For example, consider how people learn from various communicating and reporting formats of evaluation findings. Some stakeholders want to read the entire full-length final report, review all the data analyses, and perhaps even scan the raw data if they are available. Others prefer to have the results reported via a verbal presentation, where the evaluation's implementation is summarized and the key findings are discussed. Still others would rather be given a one-page summary of the evaluation's recommendations—each one bulleted. Still other stakeholders would prefer attending a debriefing or working session whereby the study can be reviewed and, through a conversation with other stakeholders, actions based on the recommendations can be explored. Although decisions about how to learn something may be influenced by the time available to do so, they also relate to how we prefer to process information. The ways in which we approach a learning task reflect our learning style preferences.

It is often helpful for people to understand their own preferred learning styles so that they can recognize the learning styles of others. For example, Brian McNulty at the Colorado Department of Education described how knowing his own learning style informs his interactions with others:

I learn by doing basically, and I jump in and muck around, and that's how I learn. Other people learn by thinking about it in very different ways. That's a wonderful set of complements. And those aren't the only two learning styles, there's a hundred of those. So when we bring people

> together where they have the permission, the freedom, the support, the encouragement, the nurturing, the whatever, to do that, it becomes a very powerful forum for what we're doing. And the issues we're dealing with are very complex. I mean, this is not making widgets. These are systems change issues. What we are dealing with is our system, but it's also school systems and it's also buildings, and it's also dealing with the public and the legislature and families. I mean, it's a very complex setting. And we've got multiple constituencies who are competing with each other to some degree, and they're at odds often times with each other. Our job is to go in and mediate these concerns and to keep things moving ahead. This is not simple answer stuff. (BM, CDE: 318)

Although being aware of an individual's learning style can be instructive, we should be cautious not to label or categorize people according to a particular mode of learning. At best, discerning individuals' learning styles opens up communication and leads to greater understanding; at its worst, it impedes communication by leading one to make broad unfounded assumptions about another person.

To summarize, adults *learn most effectively* when there is

- a perceived need for new knowledge or skills,
- an opportunity to apply what has been learned,
- an emphasis on integrating new learning with what is already known, and
- an appreciation for past experiences.

Creating the environment for individuals to learn means that organization members must

- have accurate and complete information,
- be free from coercion and distorting self-perception,
- be open to alternative perspectives,
- be able to reflect critically on presuppositions and their consequences,

- have equal opportunity to participate, and
- be able to accept an informed, objective, and rational consensus as a legitimate test of validity (Mezirow, 1991, p. 78).

TEAM LEARNING

Within organizations, individuals are always learning. It is becoming increasingly clear that this learning is maximized through opportunities to share individual knowledge and experiences with others. As work becomes more and more complex, and as the consequences of decisions and actions involve greater risks, "individual experience becomes a less reliable basis for learning" (Brooks, 1994, p. 213). An organization needs to foster teamwork, communities of practice, and other social forms of learning. "Individual talent is great, but it walks out the door. . . . Interdisciplinary teams capture, formalize, and *capitalize* talent, because it becomes shared, less dependent on any individual" (Stewart, 1997, pp. 163-164).

Learning from others is an integral part of evaluative inquiry. By bringing together people from various parts of an organization, greater insights into an evaluative issue can be attained. In describing our approach to evaluative inquiry, we have purposefully chosen to use the word *team* instead of *group* for specific reasons. A group generally is thought of as a loose association of people who may or may not share common goals and purposes. In relation to evaluative inquiry, however, a team is a special kind of group that actively works collaboratively to answer the organization's evaluative questions.

Accomplishing work objectives through teams is not always an easy task, however. In many organizations, the implementation of teams has failed because decision makers have not considered the challenges and consequences of teamwork. All too often, organizational leaders have not considered the systems and structures that are needed to support employees' involvement in teams. As we will discuss in Chapter 7, without this infrastructure, team members may find that their evaluative inquiry work does not result in the use of their learning or findings, or that the resulting actions are not supported by other organization members.

DEVELOPING TEAM CAPACITY
FOR EVALUATIVE INQUIRY

A team's ability to work together does not develop instantaneously; it does not occur without great effort, patience, and humility. Those of us who have grown up in the dominant Western, white culture repeatedly have been taught to be independent—to think and act independently. We have been told not to share our knowledge in schools— that was "cheating"—and not to share our knowledge in organizations if we want to climb the "corporate ladder." To be thrust suddenly into a teamwork situation where you are now told that shared learning is the goal requires trust in the organization, in each other, and in oneself. It also requires that we learn what it means to work together and to build the capacity of shared learning in each member. By interacting with others, we learn to change our own behaviors.

Members of evaluative inquiry teams can learn about each other's talents, similarities, and differences in several ways. One method for helping teams develop is the use of diagnostic instruments that describe different members' learning, communication, and teamwork styles, and conflict management and group process skills. These instruments can be used at the beginning of a team's development and serve to raise members' different values and worldviews that may affect their interactions with each other. For example, team members of the Prevention Initiatives unit at the Colorado Department of Education (CDE) first completed the Myers-Briggs Type Indicator (MBTI) assessment. This instrument helps individuals understand their own personality styles. Developed in the 1930s and 1940s, the MBTI, based on Carl Jung's theory of psychological type, has been researched and tested with numerous populations (Myers & McCaulley, 1985). The underlying premise of the instrument is that people all have personal preferences in the way they get energy, take in information, and make decisions. Differences in preferences cause people to communicate and behave differently. Whether team members are (a) more extroverted or introverted; (b) prefer information in the form of facts, data, and details, or theories, ideas, and relationships; (c) prefer making judgments based on objective information and logic, or subjective information and feelings, and (d) prefer closure and planning ahead, or keeping things open and flexible all influence how team members develop their capacity for engaging in evaluative inquiry. The purpose of using such instruments is not to label people but rather to acquire insights into how they prefer to think and act.

The Prevention Initiatives team also used a process called "True Colors" that helped individuals identify their work styles. As Dave Smith, Director of the Prevention Initiatives unit, explained:

I would say we were very intentional about how we developed the team. People knew that my color was blue and my secondary color was green. So I seek harmony and I'm very curious about things. When we're working well together, people will say, "Oh, that's really a blue thing for you to do." Whereas some of the people who are gold, which is a style that needs order, are more comfortable when order exists, when clear lines are drawn, when there are rules and everybody knows what those rules are. That style really is a strength when matched with my style because I tend to throw out ideas and set directions but I won't write anything down, and I might change my mind 2 days later. But working with a gold, they'll come back and say, "This is what we agreed to, and I have it all written down." And that to me is an example of two styles working together so that nobody should ever feel like they can't be a member of the team because their style is not respected. (DS, CDE: 246)

Another method for understanding how individuals prefer to learn is to pair team members and ask them to describe one of their most memorable learning experiences. They analyze the experience by describing the factors that made it so unforgettable and effective. Participants write each factor on 3 × 5 cards or sticky notes, and post them on a flipchart titled "Our Factors." The facilitator then draws connections between the factors to create a weblike chart. The web charts describe the interconnectedness of learning factors. After reviewing the factors, participants compare them with those Knowles (1980) has identified. These are respect, immediacy, relevance, and practice. Through the ensuing dialogue about Knowles' factors, team members come to understand how each person's life experiences have led to some form of learning that has shaped their values, beliefs, assumptions, and knowledge.

It is particularly important to acknowledge that all team members bring different strengths. Some people will be particularly concerned with individuals' feelings throughout the process, and will make sure no one's ideas are dismissed too quickly. Others are very good at calming down an escalating tone when things are starting to heat up. Some team members are very methodical and linear and can help keep the dialogue and inquiry process focused. Some take in information and process it more effectively away from the group, whereas others like to talk things out and make sure that enough time is spent on team processes. At the same time, other team members may prefer to focus on specific outcomes the team has been charged with accomplishing. Whereas some people are more vocal and extroverted, always adding ideas and questions to the dialogue, others are more quiet and reserved and offer periodic observations to the team. Balancing these strengths within a team can be a significant challenge for the facilitator; however, it is precisely this diversity that creates deeper and more meaningful learning from evaluative inquiry processes.

ENSURING EFFECTIVE TEAM PROCESSES FOR EVALUATIVE INQUIRY

A critical feature of effective teams is their establishment of ground rules or guidelines. Team members need to be clear about how they are expected to act—what behaviors are and are not acceptable as they work through the evaluative inquiry process. Although these ground rules help keep a team focused, they also serve as a set of procedures for handling conflict. They are the operating principles or the standards of performance that guide the team's functioning. The Prevention Initiatives team at the Colorado Department of Education calls these the "We wills" and "We wont's." As Karen Connell, a supervisor in the unit, explained, "They are agreements about how we'll act towards each other, how we'll behave and feel on behalf of the team" (KC, CDE: 340). For example, instead of assigning work to individuals who are absent from a particular meeting, the team agreed they would check with the person first before delegating such work.

Another ground rule might be making sure that all team members' opinions and perspectives are heard before developing strategies to resolve an issue. Brookfield (1995) suggests that the team think of the best and worst conversations they've ever been involved in, and discuss what made these conversations so satisfying or dissatisfying. He recommends paying particular attention to common themes, patterns, and shared experiences. Next, he advises that the team identify at least three things they could to do ensure that aspects of satisfying conversation will occur, and three things that could help avoid dissatisfying conversations.

Team members should also ask themselves, "To what standards should we hold ourselves accountable?" One way to look at such standards is to think of the dispositions the team might hope members display in their actions toward one another (see Exhibit 2.1). These are referred to as ideals because they are never fully achieved but remain the regulative norms that guide all dialogic processes (Brookfield & Preskill, in press; Preskill & Preskill, 1997). It is important that team members be provided frequent opportunities to practice them and to shape organizational relationships in the light of them. Close attention to these dispositions can go a long way toward making teams more successful.

Effective teams (Exhibit 2.2) are best facilitated by an individual who ensures that meetings are planned and carried out, that rules of dialogue are followed, that people are respectful and civilized, and that the learning processes are effectively implemented. This facilitator might be an external or internal evaluation or organization development consultant, or an employee who is recognized by others within the organization as having good facilitation and/or inquiry skills. In addition to having evaluation or inquiry skills, the facilitator should (a) be skilled in the areas of group process, collaborative problem solving, team

EXHIBIT 2.1.

*Dispositional Ideals for
Effective Team Functioning*

▲ **Hospitality** *is the manner in which people receive one another when they are genuinely committed to collaborative inquiry. Invitational in spirit, hospitality implies a mutual receptivity to new ideas and perspectives and an openness to question even the most widely accepted assumptions.*

▲ **Participation** *and efficacy are essential in any organization that strives to be both democratic and multiperspectival. Participation means that a large number of people contribute, that they do so on many different occasions with respect to many different issues, and that their contributions add depth and subtlety to the substance of the discussion. Efficacy is the sense experienced by participants that their contributions are having an impact on others, that what they have to say is valued and matters.*

▲ **Mindfulness** *emphasizes how important it is to pay attention to others, to lose oneself in hearing what someone else has to say. It also entails being aware of the whole, of who has spoken and who has not, and of doing what one can to steer collaborations in directions that are fruitful for as many people as possible.*

▲ **Humility** *is simply the willingness to admit that one's knowledge and experience are limited and incomplete and to act on that fact. It includes the acknowledgment that others have ideas that are potentially transformative and that any person in the group has a great deal to teach and to share.*

EXHIBIT 2.1.

Dispositional Ideals for Effective Team Functioning (continued)

- ▲ **Reciprocity** *means that participants care as much about others' self-development as their own and that they owe one another all the support and resources they can muster to ensure that all may pursue their individual growth and in the process greatly enhance the chances for organizational growth.*
- ▲ **Deliberation** *refers to a willingness on the part of everyone to discuss issues as fully as possible; to offer arguments and counterarguments that are supported by evidence, data, and logic; and to hold strongly to those arguments unless there are good reasons not to do so. It supports a commitment to rational discourse, but it also suggests that one enters discussion with the possibility, however remote, that the ensuing exchange of views may modify one's original opinion.*
- ▲ **Appreciation** *inclines us to express our gratitude when a helpful observation clarifies a key point or an intriguing comment excites further curiosity about an important idea. Appreciation brings people closer together and raises the level of trust. It also engenders a kind of joyous collaboration that is characteristic of the most productive and democratic organizations.*

SOURCE: Adapted from *Talking Democratically*, Brookfield and Preskill (in press). Copyright by Jossey-Bass.

development, active listening, and conflict management; (b) believe in learning as a process; and (c) model the dispositional ideals (Exhibit 2.1).

EXHIBIT 2.2.

Characteristics of Effective Teams

Effective teams:

- ▲ *Are open and honest*
- ▲ *View mistakes as opportunities to learn*
- ▲ *Have energy and enthusiasm*
- ▲ *Share information internally and externally*
- ▲ *Hold each other accountable for their actions*
- ▲ *Create a comfortable environment where humor and fun are valued*
- ▲ *Have a clear, shared purpose and direction*
- ▲ *Encourage members to challenge and support each other*
- ▲ *Establish a climate of trust*
- ▲ *Develop methods for managing and resolving conflict*
- ▲ *Encourage creativity and flexibility*
- ▲ *Have individuals who facilitate meetings that enable all the above to happen*

The facilitator strives to create a fair, open, and inclusive process that assists the team in conducting its evaluative inquiry work. Her role must be clearly defined for team members. She must make clear that her job is not to control or direct the team toward her own goals. Instead, it is to make the evaluative inquiry process easier, and free from impediments that could divert the team's purpose. As Dave Smith at CDE explained:

> I see my role really as one of facilitation more than anything else. When we can't reach consensus, I articulate that. I see it as my job to be

sensitive to the fact that we're stuck and do what is best for the team. If teams are overprocessing or underprocessing then there has to be somebody who can assess where the group is at and take responsibility for saying, "Okay, I think we need to do this and let's try this because we're stuck." It's more letting ideas evolve from the group and when there's a lack of consensus or disagreement, then it's my responsibility to remove the barrier that is impeding people from moving forward. (DS, CDE: 246)

Although one person may take the initial role of facilitation, it is possible that different team members would also facilitate at various times. Having different people facilitate meetings often strengthens the team's functioning because no one person is expected to have all the necessary skills. For example, one person might be more effective in guiding the team through a conflict than another, who is particularly adept at ensuring that all people's ideas are heard and summarized. Ultimately, all team members learn facilitation and inquiry skills by watching others model these skills. As a result, they are more likely to employ these skills during future inquiry efforts.

One caution needs to be mentioned here, however. The longer teams work together, the better individuals come to know one another. Although there are many benefits of evaluative inquiry team members becoming personally close, it also may be more difficult to hold them accountable for behaviors that obstruct the team's work. People who like one another often go along with one another's ideas to keep everyone happy. In Minnesota, people often call this "Minnesota nice." The intent here is not to hurt anyone's feelings. When we accept inappropriate things people say or do, however, we implicitly condone the action and stymie real learning from taking place. Team members must stay alert to times when their personal relationships hinder the accomplishment of meaningful work. If the team feels stuck at this point, it might be helpful to bring in another internal or external facilitator until the team gets back on track.

EXHIBIT 2.3.

Self-Monitoring Questions for Teams

▲ *How likely is it that the team's efforts will result in action? Do team members believe they are working toward accomplishing both team and organizational goals?*

▲ *To what extent do team members feel they have learned about themselves and each other as a result of the team experience? Have they changed how they think about each other?*

▲ *To what extent do team members believe the experience has enhanced their ability and willingness to work together in the future?*

▲ *To what extent do team members believe that the team process allows all voices to be heard and valued?*

▲ *How do team members feel about what they have accomplished?*

▲ *To what extent do team members believe they've made progress?*

▲ *What did team members learn in the meeting?*

An effective way for concluding a team meeting is to ask questions that focus on the group's process and progress, as described in Exhibit 2.3. It often is a good idea to capture responses to these questions in the form of minutes or notes and to distribute them later to team members. If issues were raised during this debriefing activity, they can be used to start the team's next meeting, or conversations about these issues can continue using the organization's electronic mail system.

EXHIBIT 2.4.

Characteristics of Ineffective Teams

Ineffective teams:

- ▲ *Waste time; are disorganized and inconclusive*
- ▲ *Make members feel isolated; allow individuals to dominate*
- ▲ *Have poor process facilitation*
- ▲ *Focus on irrelevant information*
- ▲ *Do not establish a clear role for team members*
- ▲ *Avoid conflict at any cost*
- ▲ *Do not value members' ideas*
- ▲ *Develop subgroups or cliques within the team*
- ▲ *Allow hidden agendas and power politics to take precedence*
- ▲ *Overemphasize process to the exclusion of content*
- ▲ *Have members who do not value teamwork*

CHALLENGES TO EFFECTIVE EVALUATIVE INQUIRY TEAMWORK

An evaluative inquiry team may not accomplish its goals or contribute to organizational learning for several reasons. Several of these can be seen in Exhibit 2.4. One threat to team learning can be the amount of time invested in meetings. If meetings are not run efficiently or productively, if they lack direction and focus, or if they are not facilitated well, individuals may feel it is not worth their time to participate. Another challenge is presented when teams include individuals who are not ready to learn collaboratively and, as a result, may not cooperate fully. Some individuals may even feel threatened by having to work with a team and may try to sabotage or interfere with the team's functioning. A third challenge has to do with the perception of organization members who are not part of the team. In organizations where teamwork is relatively new, those who are not part of a particular evaluative inquiry team may perceive that something secretive is going on during team meetings. If this fear or concern develops, the team will find itself defending its actions and will expend considerable energy dispelling rumors. Further exacerbating this problem is that evaluative inquiry team members may encounter great skepticism when they attempt to share their learning from the inquiry with others in the organization. Coworkers may be unwilling to listen to what they have to say, may refuse to discuss the issue, and may resist changing their own work behaviors. Consequently, the team's efforts to share learning from evaluative inquiry throughout the organization will be limited. When teams encounter any of these scenarios, they should raise these issues and discuss what they might do to improve the team's functioning.

MANAGING CONFLICT WITHIN
EVALUATIVE INQUIRY TEAMS

When a team engages in dialogue around an evaluative inquiry topic, eventually there will be disagreements between individuals. Team learning does not necessarily require agreement or consensus; however, how disagreements are managed is critical to the team's continued functioning. When members disagree, instead of arguing over who is right, it might be more productive to develop a means for testing the areas of disagreement. As Schwarz (1994) suggests, team members should ask themselves two questions: "How could we both be correct?" and "How could we each see the same problem differently?" (p. 50).

As anyone who has ever been part of an organization can attest, conflict is an unavoidable part of working together. Instead of seeing conflict as a barrier to learning, or as a failure to establish relationships, dialogue incorporating different viewpoints should be viewed as a method that pushes members to question existing premises—to reconceptualize their assumptions so as to create new meanings from their experiences. Although conflict is often characterized by confusion, frustration, and misunderstanding, "a group's most significant breakthroughs are often preceded by a period of struggle" (Kaner, 1996, p. 21). Nonaka and Takeuchi (1995) suggest that "it is precisely such a conflict that pushes individuals to question existing premises and to make sense of their experiences in a new way. . . . [C]onflict facilitates the transformation of personal knowledge into organizational knowledge" (p. 240).

While maintaining and accepting differences in one another, team members may come to some understanding about each other's perceptions. This appreciation also contributes to the building of a learning community described in Chapter 1. As Palmer (1987) notes, creative conflict is a primary virtue of community. He even goes so far as to suggest that "there is no knowing without conflict" (p. 25). Even when teams establish workable guidelines and develop a real sense of what each individual has to offer, conflict is unavoidable when working on complex evaluative inquiry issues. Conflict occurs because team members have different perceptions of reality based on their previous experiences, education, and background. The most critical source of conflict in teams is how they communicate with one another. How they ask for help, how they deal with problems, how differences are handled, and how their individual work styles, time pressures, and workload all contribute to the reasons conflict arises among team members. Often, team members will "attribute disagreements to personalities and fail to notice the deeper, shared assumptions" that color how individuals perceive a situation (Schein, 1996, p. 12).

Resolving such conflicts requires the ability to listen, provide feedback, give instructions, or convey information and participate in both one-on-one and group discussions (see Exhibit 2.5). Withholding judgment, acknowledging one another's contributions, dealing fairly with problems, and displaying openness—all reinforce teamwork and diffuse conflict. To ensure that conflicts are addressed before they get out of control, facilitators periodically should ask team members how they perceive the process to be going, remind members of the dispositional ideals (Exhibit 2.1), and seek peer feedback. It is particularly important to help individuals clarify their perceptions of the conflict. For example,

EXHIBIT 2.5.

Resolving Team Conflicts

To resolve team conflicts, team members must be willing to:

▲ *Listen and focus on the issue or problem, rather than on the person*

▲ *Allow some anger, frustration, or hostility to surface during the process*

▲ *Go with the process*

▲ *Accept that they themselves might be a part of the problem*

▲ *Try to change behavior*

▲ *See the issue from someone else's perspective*

▲ *Trust others' perceptions*

SOURCE: Adapted from *The Team Building Tool Kit*, Harrington-Mackin. © 1994 by the American Management Association.

is the conflict a result of one isolated event that has little to do with the whole relationship, or is it but the latest in a series of conflicts related to the quality of the relationship? Other questions worth asking are "Is the conflict really with the other person, or is it within myself?" and "Is this conflict over a difference in values or preferences, needs or desires, goals, or methods?" (Weeks, 1992). These questions help individuals focus on the source of the conflict, which may lead to a more satisfying resolution of the issue.

Conflicts that go unresolved can seriously damage the team's functioning and learning. When conflict between individuals is not addressed adequately, people begin to lose trust not only in the process but also in each other. As Beth Shober, a consultant with the Colorado Department of Education, explained:

> If you just let it grow and fester to the point that when it comes up again, it's going to be twice as bad. I don't want to go through that again. I don't want to have to continue these things where all of a sudden you never know when something's going to happen, when something erupts. I want us to go through it, get it over with, move on. (BS, CDE: 298)

When team members avoid certain topics, people, or tasks, not only will the team's effectiveness be severely diminished, but the inquiry effort will be compromised as well. Unresolved conflict impedes the sharing of ideas, information, and learning, thus blocking evaluative inquiry.

Avoiding conflict often has the effect of making small issues grow into much larger ones. The following example, from an evaluation conducted by one of the authors, shows more specifically the darker side of what happens when conflict is avoided or ignored.

Four months into the implementation of a Grade 4-8 educational reform effort, one of the school's paraprofessionals (Susan, a woman of color) overheard another paraprofessional (Janice, who is white) tell a joke that was perceived to have racial overtones. Susan was offended and asked the school's lead teacher (John) to speak to Janice about the offense. Being a person who did not like conflict, John tried to make Susan feel better and said he would talk to Janice. When John spoke to Janice and tried to persuade her to apologize privately to Susan, Janice broke down in tears and said she did not mean to offend Susan, but she did not think she had done anything wrong. Afterward, Janice felt angry and began speaking to other teachers and support staff in the school about how unfair people were being to her when she was sure the joke had not been racist. John tried to mediate the situation between Susan and Janice, and met with them individually several times. He never required the two to meet face to face, nor did he ever raise the issue of racism with the school's other teachers. Weeks went by, and eventually, months and years. The conflict between these individuals never was resolved. Soon after this incident, rumors of institutional racism began, and after 3 years, the quality of the adult relationships in the school had

deteriorated seriously. Had the issue been addressed when it first occurred, it is likely the outcome would have been much different.

In an attempt to be nice, and to make problems go away, we often do
more harm than good. Carolyn Thompson, at Presbyterian Hospital in
Albuquerque, described this kind of "benevolence" as a myth. She
suggests that we all carry around land mines (issues we have with each
other) that are buried right under the surface. Eventually, we forget that
these are buried, and at some point they explode (when we just can't
take it any more). She explained, "The problem is that they take down
not just the ground under us, but what we've built on top of it" (CT,
Pres: 209). Part of this problem is that all too often, we fail to hold
individuals responsible for their actions. Rarely do we tell someone face
to face to explain or justify their actions when they've done or said
something deemed inappropriate; nor do we stop someone from mis-
treating others in group settings. When team members hold each other
accountable, when they work through differences, they become "more
interdependent, experience higher success and express more satisfaction
with their peers than when teams are not charged with accountability
for behavior" (Fandt, 1991, p. 307).

It is when a team falls into a groupthink mentality that less learning
takes place. Groupthink occurs when a team develops a collective
pattern of thinking with members striving for unanimity instead of
exploring potentially more beneficial alternatives. It occurs most often
when team members uncritically accept the group's decision, or when
individuals do not speak up with differing opinions. Groupthink happens when a team becomes moderately or highly cohesive, feels intense
pressure and stress, and harbors illusions of invulnerability, unanimity,
and rationalization (Neck & Manz, 1994). Although group cohesiveness
and familiarity do lead to greater performance, this advantage dimin-
ishes the longer a team has been together (Guzzo & Dickson, 1996).
"Teamthink," on the other hand, leads to enhanced team performance;
it encourages divergent views and open expression of concerns and ideas,
an awareness of limitations and threats, recognition of members' unique-
ness, and discussion of collective doubts (Neck & Manz, 1994, p. 934).
In fostering teamthink, the facilitator strives to maintain a balance of
team cohesiveness while still valuing the individual. Instead of seeking

continuous consensus, the facilitator should help the team come to periodic consensus and commitment to the next steps of the evaluative inquiry process. The notion that consensus is required in collaborative efforts is a myth, according to Schrage (1989). He cites several examples of pairs or teams of individuals working collaboratively on a common goal, yet bickering or arguing frequently. Conflict "didn't preclude them from pushing ahead; . . . consensus is often irrelevant to the act or creation of discovery" (p. 161).

WHEN TEAM MEMBERS COME AND GO

As new people join an evaluative inquiry team, even if it is for a short period of time, it is vitally important that these new members be provided background on the group's history and ground rules. When new team members are not provided with this orientation, they often feel like outsiders, undervalued, confused, and frustrated by not having the same baseline information. New team members may feel embarrassed or inhibited from asking questions they think already have been asked, but for which they do not have answers. Beth Shober at CDE explained:

We've got people saying wait a minute. I don't get that. I don't understand that. And I need more explanation on that. I need someone to explain this to me. You know? And that is really hard. One of the things I've said is we have got to do a better job when people come into this unit because it is incredibly hard to come into this unit and just automatically be a member of a team. But you don't know what that team is, you don't know how they operate, you don't know what you're doing. Everybody is so busy and focused on their different stuff. (BS, CDE: 297)

As individuals come forth or are identified as being interested in working on an evaluative inquiry project, a team member should meet with them prior to their attending the next meeting. The purpose of the orientation is to provide them with a sense of the team's history and procedures. The information should include a description of the processes being used, the ground rules, members' different roles, issues the team has addressed, decisions the team has made, and some idea of what the team sees as its future direction. New members should then be given time during their first meeting with the team to ask questions of the continuing team members. The team's opportunity to reflect on the process by answering these questions may actually help the team develop new insights and perspectives on the issue being addressed, and on the team's overall functioning.

Equally important as welcoming new team members is saying goodbye to people when they feel they can no longer contribute, or when they find they can not learn any more. Sometimes this happens when an individual does not find value in teamwork and has difficulty being a "team player." Such people may have a tendency to make decisions on their own, commit others to action, or dominate discussions without letting others be heard. One's attitude toward teamwork is just as important as the skills one brings to the effort.

Often, individuals will willingly quit the inquiry team when they realize they are not fitting in, when they realize the team's expectations for team learning are not going to change and that their choice is either to adapt or to withdraw from the team. Other times, people leave the team because they believe they have contributed all they can and wish to spend their time on other initiatives. Regardless of why individuals leave, they should be able to depart in a safe, supportive way. When people leave an evaluative inquiry team knowing they have been part of something worthwhile and valued, they are more likely to share their learning with others in the organization in positive ways.

It is possible for evaluative inquiry to be carried out by one person in an organization. Inquiry that is conducted to create individual, team, and organizational learning, however, is best conducted by teams composed of a cross section of stakeholders within the organization. Through collaboratively exploring evaluative issues, team members create deeper and broader conceptions of the issue being explored. In addition, team members learn more about each other and how each person contributes to the whole of the organization. Finally, through their participation in and increased understanding of inquiry processes, they are more likely to become involved in future evaluative inquiry efforts.

HOW ORGANIZATIONS LEARN

As individuals and teams share their learning from evaluative inquiry with others, it can be said that the organization learns. By applying the results of evaluative inquiry to pressing organizational issues, organizations can improve their practices, processes, products, and services. Although the work on organizational learning was introduced in the management theory literature by Argyris and Schon (1978) two decades ago, the concept was made popular and accessible by Peter Senge's book *The Fifth Discipline* (1990a) published over a decade ago. Since that time, dozens of books and articles have described how organizations can and should become learning organizations.

In response to changes in the economy and workforce, and to an interest in building learning communities, many organizations have implemented organizational learning practices and processes. For example, we learned from our field research that the Electrical Fuel and Handling Division (EFHD) of Ford Motor Company developed an introductory 5-day course on the learning organization with a local community college. In the course, participants (who include hourly and salaried employees as well as vendors) learn the basic concepts of organizational learning. The course is offered several times a year. In addition, the EFHD uses "strategic dialogue" as a learning tool for team learning. On an ongoing basis, teams come together to engage in an open conversation about the issues facing the plant and how they might do things differently. The division's Operating Committee also meets once a week to discuss specific issues to come to a better understanding of the problems and potential solutions. All these efforts contribute to the division's desire to be a learning organization.

Results from a survey conducted of human resource development executives by the American Society for Training and Development (ASTD, 1996b) show that 57% of the respondents think that becoming a learning organization is "very important" or "important." When asked if they planned to take steps to make their's become a learning organi-zation in the next year, 45% said "yes," 40% responded "no," and 15% said they "don't know." Amazingly, 60% of the respondents said the number one barrier to becoming a learning organization is that there is "no clear understanding of organizational learning" in their organization!

Although many writers and practitioners use the terms *organizational learning* and *learning organization* interchangeably, there are differences worth noting. When we talk about learning organizations, we focus on the what, and describe systems, principles, and charac-teristics of organizations that learn as collective entities. Organiza-tional learning, however, refers to "how organizational learning oc-curs, that is, the skills and processes of building and utilizing knowledge" (Marquardt, 1996a, p. 19). It is particularly concerned with the ways in which learning is created and shared. For example:

> Organizations learn through joint discussion and interpretation of events, and through gradual changes in the assumptions, symbols, and values of participants. In this approach, trials and errors, or actions and outcomes, are important means of learning. (Daft & Huber, 1987, p. 10)

Fiol and Lyles (1985) define organizational learning as changes in the organization's cognition or behavior. Learning is "the development of insights, knowledge, associations between past actions, the effectiveness of those actions, and future action" (p. 811). Change, or adaptation, as the authors call it, is "the ability to make incremental adjustments as a result of environmental changes, goal structure changes, or other changes" (p. 811). This approach takes a developmental stance in its view of how organizations change.

For some, the thought of an organization learning is impossible—how could something that is not living, learn? Argyris and Schon (1996) believe that "by establishing rule governed ways of deciding, delegating, and setting the boundaries of membership, a collective becomes an organization capable of action" (p. 9). These organizations "act on a continuing basis over time, and thus, build up systems, policies, procedures, and cultures" (Marsick & Neaman, 1996, p. 98). When individuals inquire into a problematic situation on the organization's behalf (Argyris & Schon, 1996, p. 16) and "retain, crystallize, or embed new practices, values, or understandings" (Watkins, 1996, p. 90), the organization learns. This learning takes place at a systems level that is fueled by organization members' intellectual capital, memories, experiences, knowledge, routines, and competencies (Gephart, Marsick, Van Buren, & Spiro, 1996). Organizational learning represents the organization's commitment to using all of its members' capabilities. In this respect, it is different from individual and team learning; organizational learning is dependent on individuals and teams sharing their learning in an ongoing, systemic way. Evaluative inquiry provides the organization a means for (a) developing a community of inquirers, (b) harnessing the knowledge capital of its members, and (c) addressing problematic issues that face the organization. It serves as a catalyst for learning and action on organizational issues.

Those we interviewed in our field research described that in practice, organizational learning is manifested in how an organization functions and succeeds. In addition, it is seen as a means of supporting individual and team activities and goals. The following definitions were provided by our interviewees.

▲ I interpret organizational learning as a conscientious focus on our intellectual capital, intellectual assets in a way that will help people acquire the capabilities and skills, competencies they need to contribute to the organization; and that we identify learning needs built around business needs and create learning plans that will result in the kind of learning that we need for the organization. (JM, LOL: 188)

▲ I see it [a learning organization] as an organization that's just as simple as possible, open to learning, open to growing, open to people who handle change and are always wanting to explore new things and are always finding other avenues to do things. (DF, LOL: 112)

▲ I think what the learning organization does is help people master the disciplines of openness, honesty and trust and surfaces the mental models. It destroys all the obstacles and barriers, it allows us to spend all our energy focusing on making the best-of-class products and best-of-class parts. And being a learning organization prevents us, prohibits us, from spending any kind of time protecting our turf, kissing our bosses' asses or back stabbing. (DB, Ford: 78)

▲ Organizational learning means that people think differently and work differently together; think differently in terms of being aware of their own thought processes and how they react to situations and how they fit in broader context. The other piece of it is that the organization as a whole is taking knowledge and expertise and information and lessons learned in one place, and saying, "how do we apply this over here so we don't re-create the wheel?" So to me it has some tactical meaning in terms of applying learnings across areas that generally haven't talked or don't work together. (BS, Pres: 224)

So, in many respects, all organizations learn—but how they learn, why they learn, what they learn, and how they apply their learning varies significantly. For instance, some organizations repeatedly make the same mistakes, failing to improve their services or to meet customers' or clients' needs and expectations. These organizations tend to adapt to new requirements quickly, often without much intentional thought or planning. Other organizations are more committed to learning about what the problems are and explore different solutions before making changes. An organization's approach to learning has been described as single-loop, double-loop, and deutero learning (Argyris & Schon, 1978, 1996; Bateson, 1972). Single-loop learning, also referred to as instrumental learning, results in a change of strategy or action, yet leaves intact the values of a theory of action. In other words, people's assumptions underlying the actions remain unchanged and unquestioned. It is the kind of learning used to maintain the status quo and is often employed in crisis situations. Single-loop learning typically results in short-term solutions to organizational problems. We have seen this type of learning repeatedly over the last 30 years as organizations have adopted many of the highly visible innovations discussed in Chapter 1. Organizations have latched onto the latest fad without carefully considering the actions and consequences of how it will be integrated into its current practices, policies, systems, or culture (see Chapter 7). The organization merely reacts instead of engaging in an evaluative inquiry process to determine what it might take to make such a change.

An example of single-loop learning is a school district that is dissatisfied with the level of students' test scores. District administrators decide that the current standardized test is not measuring students' learning of the district's curriculum and thus chooses to administer a different standardized test. Although action was taken to change the test, there was no inquiry into the values, beliefs, assumptions, or knowledge of standardized testing as an appropriate and necessary method of measuring student achievement. The values and norms underlying the use of standardized testing remained unchanged. This kind of action results in an incremental change that continues to reinforce the district's existing goals.

Continuing with the testing example, let's now assume that a group of people come together to explore the overall issue of the district's testing policy and procedures. Under discussion is not just the use of this one test that does not seem to produce the desired test scores but also the district's overall approach to student assessment (double-loop learning). First, the team identifies questions that clarify the issue and how it might be resolved. Then members engage in a dialogue that helps them identify their values, beliefs, assumptions, and knowledge around the issue of testing, using a process of question-asking and reflection. Then they decide to collect, analyze, and interpret data related to their questions. As a result of this evaluative inquiry process, they come to realize that the forms of testing the district uses are inconsistent with the values and assumptions they have about measuring student achievement. They decide that the district must fundamentally change its approach to student testing. They begin a process to change the norms and assumptions that have guided the use of standardized testing in their district, and to develop alternative forms of measuring student achievement that more closely resemble the district's values, beliefs, assumptions, and knowledge about student learning.

On the other hand, deutero learning is what many educators are striving to develop in both children and adults today. It focuses on learning how to learn. Given the constant change in organization's structures, individuals' roles in organizations, and the nature of work, learning how to learn is fast becoming a critical competency for organizational survival. In the context of organizational learning, learning how to learn refers to organization members reflecting on their own and the team's learning processes. It requires people to step back and, using an inquiry approach, consider what helped or hindered the learning approach taken to solve the problem or address the issue. From this inquiry process, new strategies for learning are developed for future use.

What organizations choose to focus their learning on also varies significantly. For example, organizations can learn how to improve current processes or existing skills; this kind of learning is an attempt to solve some issue or problem. Take, for example, a team of middle school teachers who engage in evaluative inquiry to better understand how they can eliminate the development of student cliques. They have noticed that many students are being left out of in-school and out-of-school activities, that student morale appears to be declining, and that there has been an increase in verbal attacks on students of different cliques. From the evaluative inquiry, they hope to learn how to decrease the number of cliques and improve how students feel about being in school.

Organizations that *learn why* are interested in developing interpersonal competence (Argyris, 1985; Moingeon & Edmondson, 1996). Once individuals are aware of the disjuncture between what they say and what they do, they are able to modify their thinking processes and resulting behaviors. This kind of learning often results in the creation of organization level structures, strategies, and policies. For example, consider a computer hardware company that advertises its technical customer service as the most friendly, responsive, and timely, and that its technicians are the "most experienced in the field." In the last 6 months, however, the vice president of customer service has received numerous verbal and written comments from customers expressing concern that they have had to wait up to 1 month for service, that they have been left holding on the phone for up to 1 hour, and that when finally they have been able to reach a "real" person, the technician on the phone "did not have a clue" about how to help them. An organization experiencing this kind of issue might engage evaluative inquiry to better understand the disjuncture between what the company advertises and the current quality of customer service. The inquiry team would focus on the underlying values of how the company advertises as well as the values that undergird its philosophy of customer service. As a result of the inquiry, the organization might either change its advertising approach or decide to hire additional, as well as more highly experienced, technicians. The results of the evaluative inquiry might also indicate a need to provide opportunities for technicians to share their learning with others.

What they learn refers to what individuals and teams choose to focus on learning from the evaluative inquiry effort. Do they look at one symptom of a larger problem, intent on fixing only that which appears most troublesome (single-loop learning), or do they delve deeper into an issue, seeking to understand the underlying causes and consequences (double-loop learning)? For example, suppose a nonprofit organization has been experiencing significant turnover in its volunteer staff. A team of staff members and current volunteers comes together to engage in evaluative inquiry to look at the reasons for the high turnover. They could focus on one aspect of turnover, such as how well the volunteers are trained to do their work, or they could look more broadly at issues such as administrative support, coaching and feedback, expectations for volunteers, and workload. If they choose only to explore how volunteers may be better trained, they may or may not be focusing on the real issue of why volunteers leave the agency. If they choose to look at a wider set of variables, they are more likely to discover the underlying reasons for the high volunteer turnover. This broader focus for the evaluative inquiry leads to deeper and more meaningful learning about the issue.

Why they learn has to do with what the organization hopes to achieve by developing a systemwide learning culture. An organization may have *pragmatic* or instrumental reasons for learning, such as developing competitive advantage. Learning may be perceived as an *evolutionary* process that helps the organization respond to changing environmental circumstances, such as global competition, or as just plain survival. An organization also may want to learn for *aspirational* reasons. Such aspirations include the desire to develop a worldwide learning community with an emphasis on dialogue and cooperative processes that build and sustain organizational harmony (Binns, 1994; Burgoyne, 1992;

Leitch, Harrison, & Burgoyne, 1996). As we learned in our field research, companies such as Presbyterian Healthcare Services, Land O' Lakes, and the EFHD Division of Ford are implementing organizational learning practices in response to increased competition. They have very pragmatic reasons to change—survival. Having organization members build evaluative inquiry into ongoing work processes, however, can help organizations address not only their pragmatic questions but their aspirational needs as well. For example, a business might wish to understand more fully how it can contribute to its local community's economic health, or how it can help better prepare students for their entry into the labor market. In either of these two situations, organization and community members might engage in evaluative inquiry to explore how these goals can be achieved.

MODELS OF ORGANIZATIONAL LEARNING

In the last decade, a number of models describing the linkages between individual, team, and organizational learning have been developed. In their book *Creating the Learning Organization* (1996), Watkins and Marsick provide 22 case examples of organizations that have attempted to establish organizational learning systems. Looking across these examples and others from the research literature, they conclude that most models share the following attributes:

- Learning organizations focus on organizational learning and transformation; it is not enough for individuals to learn.
- Structures and systems are created to ensure that knowledge is captured and shared for use in the organization's memory.
- Leaders and employees at all levels think systematically about the impact of their decisions and work within the total system.
- Learning is built into work structures, politics, and practices.
- Learning is transformative in some way, although it is likely that some new learning will also be adaptive.

- Learning has a greater impact when it involves a greater percentage of the employee population.
- Organizational systems and policies are structured to support, facilitate, and reward learning for individuals, teams, and the organization.
- New measurement systems benchmark current knowledge and culture and monitor progress toward becoming a learning organization (p. 10).

The majority of organizational learning models focus on learning as a change process, one that seeks to involve all of its employees in an effort to harness their intellectual capacity and knowledge capital for the purpose of individual, team, and organizational growth. It also can be seen as a "continuous process of organizational growth and improvement that: (a) is integrated with work activities, (b) invokes the alignment of values, attitudes, and perceptions among organizational members, and (c) uses information or feedback about both processes and outcomes to make changes" (Torres et al., 1996, p. 2). It is important to note that learning in organizations is nonlinear, open, and constantly evolving to higher levels of complexity (Schwandt, 1995).

In summary, evaluative inquiry for organizational learning and change is grounded in a social constructivist theory of learning which suggests that learning takes place through (a) the collective creation of meaning, (b) action, (c) the development of new knowledge, (d) an improvement in systemic processes, and (e) the overcoming of tacit assumptions. Team learning from evaluative inquiry occurs when individuals share their experiences, values, beliefs, assumptions, and knowledge through dialogue, and engage in collaborative learning efforts. When individuals and teams disseminate their learning from inquiry throughout an organization, and action results from this learning, it can be said that the organization learns. Evaluative inquiry can facilitate learning at all levels by stimulating and supporting the ongoing process of asking ques-

tions, the collection and analysis of data, and using what is learned from an inquiry to act on important organizational issues. What follows in Chapter 3 is a discussion of the four learning processes that facilitate individual, team, and organizational learning from evaluative inquiry.

Evaluative Inquiry Learning Processes

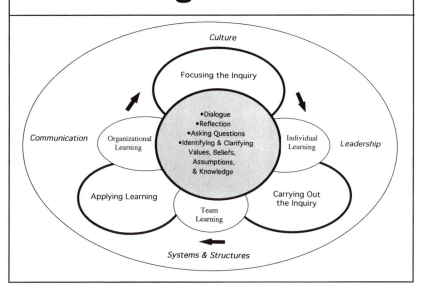

In the two previous chapters, we have discussed how organizations are changing and the need for them to develop the learning capacity of their employees. In this chapter, we describe four learning processes that facilitate three phases of evaluative inquiry: *Focusing the Evaluative Inquiry* (Chapter 4), *Carrying Out the*

Inquiry (Chapter 5), and *Applying Learning* (Chapter 6). In the *focusing the inquiry* phase, team members determine what issues and concerns the evaluative effort will address, who the stakeholders are, and what questions will guide the evaluative inquiry. In the next phase, *carrying out the inquiry*, organization members design and implement the inquiry by collecting, analyzing, and interpreting data that address the evaluative questions. They also develop recommendations and communicate and report the inquiry's processes and findings. During the third phase, *applying learning*, organization members identify and select action alternatives, develop and implement action plans, and monitor their progress.

As each of the inquiry phases is implemented, organization members come together to engage in the learning processes of (a) *Dialogue*, (b) *Reflection*, (c) *Asking Questions*, and (d) *Identifying and Clarifying Values, Beliefs, Assumptions, and Knowledge*. Dialogue is the fuel for energizing these learning processes, whereas the processes themselves are the vehicles for learning throughout the inquiry effort. We have chosen to label these activities as *learning processes* to communicate the spirit of evaluative inquiry. As defined by Webster's *Third New International Dictionary*, the word "process" is "the action of moving forward progressively from one point to another on the way to completion; the action of passing through continuing development from a beginning to a contemplated end." It is important to note that we do not view these processes as linear, though one might easily conclude that from the above definition. For example, individuals do not necessarily first reflect, then ask questions, and then identify their own values and beliefs. Rather, these learning processes occur through a dynamic, fluid, social interaction among organizational members.[1] Through these processes, evaluative inquiry provides the means for learning and action that results in ongoing individual, team, and organizational growth and development.

DIALOGUE

Through dialogue, individuals seek to inquire, share meanings, understand complex issues, and uncover assumptions. In other words, dialogue is what facilitates the evaluative inquiry learning processes of reflection, asking questions, and identifying and clarifying values, beliefs, assumptions, and knowledge. Through dialogue, individuals make connections with each other and communicate personal and social understandings that guide subsequent behaviors. As David Berdish from Ford Motor Company explains:

> We have meetings to dialogue and reflect on how we're doing, what we're doing, and what we need to do. It's action oriented to fix our processes and to create a better future for ourselves. (DB, Ford: 70)

Dialogue facilitates individuals' learning about the organization's culture, policies, procedures, and goals and objectives. It is the cognitive "place" where practitioners may confront contradictions that otherwise might go unchallenged and unquestioned. It is also where group members can agree, at least for a while, to suspend judgment in order to create new understandings. Dialogue has been defined as

> *a sustained collective inquiry into everyday experience and what we take for granted.* The goal of dialogue is to open new ground by establishing a "container" or "field" for inquiry, a setting where people can become more aware of the context around their experience, and of the processes of thought and feeling that created that experience. (Senge, Roberts, Ross, Smith, & Kleiner, 1994, p. 353)

Although the terms "discussion" and "dialogue" are often used interchangeably, there are differences worth noting. Dialogue can be thought of as "*a stream of meaning* flowing among and through us and between us" where the goal is a spirit of understanding, not competition of ideas (Bohm, 1996, p. 6). Discussion, on the other hand, comes from the same root words as "percussion" and "concussion," which means to break apart—to break down into analytic parts (Bohm, 1996, p. 7). For example, the purpose of discussion is to tell, sell, or persuade. It is an attempt to find agreement, defend one's assumptions, or convince someone of an idea—the result being a sense of having "won" the argument. Discussion is often about preserving the status quo. On the other hand, dialogue is about communities and learning for change. It empowers people to be heard, allows agendas to be made public, and facilitates individual, team, and organizational learning. Through the sharing of individuals' personal knowledge, dialogue has the potential to build capacities that dissolve resistance in times of organizational upheaval (Brown, 1995). Asking for reasons behind statements, questions, and actions further helps individuals weigh the pros and cons of different opinions, thereby enabling them to achieve greater levels of understanding. Because of organization members' varied backgrounds and experiences, individuals must engage in dialogue to identify resources and to understand, accept, and appreciate each other's differences so that they can accomplish both personal and organizational goals. In this vein, dialogue contributes to the production of new knowledge that can be shared between and among team members (Brooks, 1994).

Engaging in dialogue brings several benefits (Exhibit 3.1). As individuals communicate and comprehend each other's viewpoints, they assimilate pieces that fit with their own experience and way of thinking. This often results in a negotiated, new perspective that contains elements of both persons' thoughts. Dialogue also helps individuals deal with errors in thinking that cause them to generate faulty conclusions on which they base their behavior. Common types of thinking error are (a) personalization, (b) overgeneralization, and (c) polarization. Personalization refers to the tendency to relate all people and events to oneself. Overgeneralization is the tendency to make broad, generalized conclusions based on a single incident or piece of information. Polarization is the tendency to see things as right or wrong, or black or white, with no middle ground (Phillips & Phillips, 1995). Dialogue has the potential to make these distortions public and explicit, thereby allowing a group to correct them. Dialogue not only requires the suspension of defensive responses but also looks into the reasons for such defensiveness.

Dialogue offers opportunities to identify possible barriers to inquiry and potential misuses of the evaluative inquiry processes and outcomes. In addition, dialogue enables "undiscussable" issues to be addressed in an open and honest way. In every organization, there are topics that

EXHIBIT 3.1.

Benefits of Dialogue

▲ *Brings to the surface multiple points of view that need to be addressed and negotiated*
▲ *Helps make individual and hidden agendas visible*
▲ *Allows team members to develop shared meanings that are important for further inquiry activities*
▲ *Contributes to building a sense of community and connection*
▲ *Illuminates the organization's culture, policies, and procedures*
▲ *Increases the likelihood that learning at the team level will lead to learning throughout the organization*
▲ *Enables undiscussables to surface and be addressed*
▲ *Facilitates individual, team, and organizational learning*

employees hesitate voicing in meetings, usually for fear of being punished or marginalized. These topics might include discriminatory practices, ineffective management policies, mismatches between what executives say and actually do, or inappropriate employee expectations. When dialogue processes are supported by the organization's infrastructure (Chapter 7), the undiscussables can become discussable. No longer are certain topics off limits. Instead, dialogue is viewed as a means to learn and to acquire greater appreciation and understanding of why certain topics have been avoided. Questions addressing the undiscussables might include

- What is the threat behind the undiscussable?
- How does this undiscussable affect our ability to learn?
- What has kept this issue from being discussed?
- What haven't we asked about the issue?

It is quite possible that when these topics are discussed, they can be dealt with through an evaluative inquiry process.

Bringing people together through dialogue helps them see that they are not alone in their thinking and that they need not solve problems in isolation. As Mariann Bischoff, from Ford Motor Company, explained:

I don't have to sit at my desk and solve a problem. In fact, that's rarely the way it happens. There's so much more when you meet with a whole bunch of different people who have different knowledge in the different areas and you talk the thing out, and the solution comes out of that dialogue. (MB, Ford: 33)

As individuals understand commonalities of experience through dialogue, they may be more creative in developing solutions to organizational challenges.

REFLECTION

Reflection is a process that enables individuals and groups to review their ideas, understandings, and experiences. Reflection enables team members to explore each other's values, beliefs, assumptions, and knowledge related to the issue of interest (see Exhibit 3.2). When we understand individuals' mental models (e.g., images, stories, points of view), we begin to understand how two people can observe the same event yet describe it differently. Given our varied backgrounds and experiences, we are prone to focus on different details of these experiences. In most cases, however, how we make sense of the world remains unexplored, tacit, and untested. Reflection is central to sustaining evaluative inquiry efforts.

Over the last 60 or so years, many writers have offered definitions of what it means to engage in reflection (e.g., Brookfield, 1995; Dewey, 1933; Mezirow, 1991). Mezirow (1991) suggests there are three types or foci of reflection. The first, *content reflection*, refers to reflection on the

EXHIBIT 3.2.

Benefits of Reflection

▲ *Enables team members to think more deeply and holistically about an issue, leading to greater insights and learning*

▲ *Connects the rational decision-making process to a more affective and experiential learning process*

▲ *Challenges individuals to be honest about the relationship between what they say and what they do*

▲ *Creates opportunities to seriously consider the implications of any past or future action*

▲ *Acts as a safeguard against making impulsive decisions*

content or description of a problem or issue. The second, *process reflection*, involves analyzing the methods and strategies that are being used to resolve the problem. The third type of reflection is *premise reflection*. This type asks us to consider why the problem is a problem in the first place.

Unfortunately however, barriers to reflection permeate the work environment. These barriers include "performance pressure" (time for reflection is a luxury and ill-afforded), competency traps (it is quicker and easier to keep doing what we are already doing even if it is not in the best interests of the organization), and absence of learning forums or structures (the leadership and culture do not reward learning) (Shaw & Perkins, 1991). An example of a performance pressure barrier was provided by Mark Wilberts, vice president of information systems at Land O' Lakes, who firmly believes in reflection as a tool for organizational learning and has trained his team in a reflection process. He laments the fact that his employees are so busy they have not had time to reflect on their work. He explains:

Part of the problem we have right now is everybody is so busy that to take time out to reflect, it's almost a burden because now I've got to work after hours or another Saturday morning to get my job done. We have been for 2 years under the gun—task, task, task. That's the biggest reason. And we just plain haven't taken the time. (MW, LOL: 367)

A perceived lack of time results in part from the larger organizational culture, which has not yet made the shift from short-term to long-term thinking and has not established a learning culture. Yet the value of critical reflection can not be overlooked:

To learn from our experiences we must become competent in taking action while simultaneously reflecting on that action. To effectively initiate, implement, and sustain transformation, we must reflect on the values behind our actions. We must be willing to reflect critically on what we are doing. Theories should guide practice, and then practice should inform theory. We should always be learning and analyzing as a way of organizational life. (Mink et al., 1994, p. 8)

When organization members reflect on their beliefs and resultant actions, they begin to understand how and why things happen the way they do. When they engage in reflection with others, they can gather more information with which to interpret their own experiences. Reflection enables us to interpret individual behavior within a holistic framework by seeing how our own behavior is affected by others and, at the same time, how our own behavior affects other organization members. Reflection has been known to prompt changes in self-concept or in perception of an event or a person, and it has been used as a planning tool for changing behavior (Canning, 1991).

Reflection can stimulate inquiry and learning at various times and in various ways. Reflection may occur while engaged in an activity, at the completion of the activity, or for future activities. Reflection while we are engaged in some task occurs when we watch ourselves as we act out certain thoughts and actions. It is often like standing outside or beside ourselves, watching what we are doing from a different perspective. An example is the trainer or teacher who constantly monitors and assesses how well the program is going and makes adjustments as she goes along. Reflection that takes place after we have completed a task provides opportunities to revisit or recall what occurred in practice. Reflection on underlying premises challenges individuals to consider the mental models, assumptions, and knowledge that influenced their practice. Finally, reflection for future action or practice focuses on predicting how we will use what we learned in the reflection process (Saban, Killion, & Green, 1994; Schon, 1983, 1987; Schwandt, 1995).

To engage practitioners in reflection, Saban and colleagues (1994) suggest that participants adopt a centrist point of view. That is, group members are guided through a process in which they apply (a) *egocentrism*, where actions are explored or examined from the perspective of the individual; (b) *allocentrism*, where participants see the world and consider actions, experiences, or events from someone else's point of view; and (c) *macrocentrism*, where the focus is on how the system or organization might view certain actions, events, or experiences. Team members then develop questions for each other that represent these viewpoints and encourage members to share their thoughts.

For example, an evaluative inquiry team has concluded from its inquiry work that a community-based health care education program should be implemented in rural and underserved communities. The team has decided to design and develop an education and awareness program that informs community members about its services. To ensure that it develops the most effective program, the team decides to reflect on its choices and decisions as it designs the program. For each of the design components, team members ask themselves, "How do I react to this design element?" (egocentrism), "How might community members respond to this program design element?" (allocentrism), and "What might health care providers think about this aspect of the design?" (macrocentrism). By reflecting on the program's design from several perspectives, the team is able to uncover differing values, beliefs, and assumptions that guide thinking about the program's design. Exploring these perspectives leads to an increased likelihood that the program will meet the needs of the community members and health care providers.

We have discussed the importance of reflection when team members are together, but it is important to remember that reflection also occurs during the "in-between" times when team members are not at work or in a team meeting. We have all had these reflective occurrences while driving, washing dishes, gardening, or just staring out the office window. Methods to stimulate these individual reflections include meditation, journal writing, and spontaneous thinking during rhythmic activity such as walking, running, or swimming. To make sure these insights are not lost, it is useful to begin team meetings by asking members what they have been thinking about since the last meeting.

The reflection process helps us come to know and understand ourselves. Knowing ourselves is critical to creating new meanings that lead to personal development and change. Engaging in critical reflection as a group develops an even stronger community of practice.

ASKING QUESTIONS

"*Asking the proper question is the central act of transformation . . .*" (Chawla, 1995, p. 505); asking questions is a fundamental characteristic of organizations that learn. It is also one of the first tasks of any evaluative inquiry project. Asking questions, however, has not been highly valued in many organizations' cultures. Too often, asking questions has been seen as a means of challenging authority, evading someone else's question, or placing blame. After analyzing the taped conversations of executive meetings, Ryan (1995) found that few questions had been asked in several hours of meetings. She asks, *"What if we valued the questions we hear as much as the answers we worship in our allocation of time?"* (p. 282). The point is that when we fail to ask questions, we lose the opportunity to acquire information, insight, clarity, and direction that would resolve problems more efficiently and effectively. In short, we miss out on learning at deeper levels (see Exhibit 3.3).

Examples of not asking questions can be seen in any organizational environment where people leap from the problem to the solution without questioning what happened. In business organizations, we see the lack of questioning when introducing new programs such as Total

EXHIBIT 3.3.

Benefits of Asking Questions

▲ *Identifies issues of key importance to the organization*
▲ *Acknowledges employees' prior knowledge*
▲ *Uncovers a broad range of issues on which to focus an inquiry*
▲ *Develops a culture of curiosity and a spirit for inquiry*
▲ *Challenges organization members' current knowledge and understanding*
▲ *Stimulates continuous learning*
▲ *Leads to deeper levels of understanding and knowledge*

Quality Management and Business Process Reengineering. As described in Chapter 1, these programs often are embraced with great fanfare, then within 1 or 2 years are dismissed as failures with no one knowing how, why, and in what ways they may have failed. We see it in organizations' training departments where trainers are asked to design and develop training programs without conducting needs assessments. In our schools, educators have too often determined that a school's curriculum should be built around Howard Gardner's (1983) multiple intelligences model without carefully considering the implications and consequences of such a curriculum. In evaluation practice, evaluators see it when, at the beginning of an evaluation, the client suggests conducting a survey without having clearly identified the purpose, stakeholders, and expected uses of the inquiry's findings. Not asking questions leads to action without thought. Carolyn Thompson of Presbyterian Hospital notes that those who have attained positions of authority often have succeeded by being the most verbal. She suggests that discussion has been relegated "to a battle of words rather than to a battle of questions" (CT, Pres: 207).

In an effort to help organization members develop questioning skills, Garvin (1984, p. 20) offers the following typology of questions:

- Broad diagnostic questions that provide a stimulus for opening up discussion, such as "What's your interpretation (of a given situation)?" and "What's the problem?"
- Specific questions of "action or decision" that ask practitioners what they should or would do in a given situation.
- Questions of extension or synthesis, such as "How does that comment tie in (with someone else's comment)?" or "What are the implications (of someone else's comment)?"
- Questions of priority or ranking, such as "What's the most important issue?"
- Questions that challenge and test, such as "Do you really believe that?" or that ask for evidence to support a claim.
- Simple questions of clarification, such as "What do you mean by that?"
- Factual "fill-in-the-blank" kinds of questions.
- Hypothetical questions, such as "Suppose that instead of being the smallest company, the firm were the largest—would that change your recommendations in any way?"
- Summary questions, such as "What themes or lessons have emerged from this discussion?"

As organizations continue to change and evolve, the cost of not asking questions will increase. Organizations can no longer afford to offer products and services without knowing the extent of their effectiveness. No longer can senior management rely solely on gut feelings and information from their inner circle to make decisions. Organizations that survive will be those that have cultures that support asking the hard questions and have developed methods, processes, and systems to answer those questions. In *The Web of Inclusion* (1995), Sally Helgeson describes how Dan Wolf, who founded and edited the *Village Voice* newspaper in the early 1970s, "shaped the organization by listening and asking the right questions, eliciting ideas that people hadn't even known they had" (p. 6). Some believe that the success of the paper was due largely to how employees were made to feel a part of the decision-making process. As Helgeson explains:

> This approach made everyone involved with the paper feel like participants in the debate and part of something important and always evolving. A kind of fractious togetherness developed, a good example of what *Inc.* magazine has recently called "emancipation capitalism," an enterprise in which everyone who is part of it feels a sense of ownership—even if, in literal terms, they have none. (p. 7)

Even when questions are asked in organizations today, employees find that there is a strong tendency to believe that expert knowledge resides somewhere other than within the organization itself. Although this tendency has created vast opportunities for external consultants who make a living by providing advice to organizations, it has had serious consequences for those within organizations who possess expertise that goes untapped. By underutilizing employees, we create cultures of apathy, lethargy, and anti-learning. The truth is, we have failed to tap the potential of organization members' knowledge and experience. We have not asked organization members what they know, do not know, and need to know, before seeking outside assistance. As manager David Berdish at Ford Motor Company explained:

I think one of our biggest learning disabilities is that if you're a salaried graded 8 engineer for 20 years, then you're worthless. Maybe that person has been there 20 years and has the knowledge that no one will ever learn if we don't tap it. (DB, Ford: 75)

Although there are times when it is necessary and valuable to engage a consultant to add expertise, we have too often overlooked the knowledge, skills, and experiences of people closest to the problem. On the other hand, there are times we are too quick to assume that we "know" something fully when in fact we hold only a piece of the puzzle. The tendency not to acknowledge the limits of our own knowledge has been referred to as pre-reflective reasoning (King & Kitchener, 1994). Such reasoning is characterized by individuals asserting that what they have seen is true, and what they have perceived is all that exists. Although there may be several intellectual and ethical reasons for this kind of reasoning, there are also organizational barriers that limit question asking in organizations. As Julie Tschida, a human resources consultant at Land O' Lakes, acknowledged:

> We rarely talk about what it is we don't know and need to learn. We talk about everything we know. I suppose this is because there's a fear that we'll look stupid. It has been rare to hear our top management say, "I don't know the answer to that." However, as we continue our journey towards becoming a learning organization, it is becoming less rare. Admitting "I don't know," no longer carries the severe negative connotation it once did. (JT, LOL: 178)

Ginger Juncker at Ford Motor Company added, "There's not a lot of places where you're rewarded for saying, 'I don't know.' It's typically you either know or you fake it, or say, 'I'll get back to you on that' " (GJ, Ford: 100). In fact, some believe that in many organizations, people's careers would be jeopardized if they admitted they did not know something. David Berdish at Ford provided the following example to illustrate this point:

> If my boss asks me about something and I said I don't know, I'd get shellacked and probably my career is grounded. You don't know. Well, the first thing you have to admit if you want to learn something is say you don't know. And that takes a lot of guts. I mean, we're not rewarded for saying you don't know. (DB, Ford: 61)

Asking questions about individuals' knowledge and experience is an important method for exploring the capacity of organization members.

As Mary Vanderwall at the Colorado Department of Education suggests, "Asking questions is one of the ways we get beyond where we've always been" (MV, CDE: 266). More and more organizations are beginning to find ways to capture the expertise of their employees. At Fortune magazine, when employees retrieve their e-mail each day, they typically see the message, "Does anyone know . . .?" The editor explains that this is part of a trend at the magazine to "accumulate the knowledge of individual employees into an organizational asset" (Allerton, 1996, p. 8).

Asking questions as "inquiry practitioners" (Argyris & Schon, 1996) and "communities of inquirers" (Ryan, 1995) develops a spirit of curiosity that serves as a catalyst for learning. As many researchers, evaluators, and consultants have witnessed, the mere asking of a survey or interview question can cause individuals to change their thinking or practice, even when personal enlightenment was not the inquiry's goal. Good questions awaken curiosity, challenge our limited views, and create opportunities for dynamic learning. Postman and Weingartner (1969) remind us, "Once you have learned how to ask questions—relevant and appropriate and substantial questions—you have learned how to learn and no one can keep you from learning whatever you want to need to know" (p. 23).

Ultimately, the kinds of questions organization members should be asking are questions that bring them closer to achieving the organization's mission and goals. We all should be asking what, where, how, when, and why questions of all we do. Most of the time, these questions will emerge as a result of a problem, issue, or concern employees have about a particular program, process, product, service, policy, or procedure. These questions are not the type that typically lead to yes or no answers or one correct answer. Rather, these questions are truly open-ended and require a dialogic process that supports the collection of information covering a wide range of possible actions. Only by asking questions can real change occur.

Evaluative inquiry requires that people carefully consider their current level of knowledge and understanding about the problem or issue at hand and determine what other information is needed. The consistent and ongoing questioning about the practices, processes, and outcomes of our work stimulates continuous learning, a sense of connectedness, and improved individual, team, and organizational performance. At the end of the book a list of questions relevant to facilitating each phase of the evaluative inquiry process is provided (see Chapters 4, 5, and 6).

IDENTIFYING AND CLARIFYING VALUES, BELIEFS, ASSUMPTIONS, AND KNOWLEDGE

As people come together to engage in dialogue and reflection around an issue of concern, their opinions, perceptions, and views of the world become operationalized. These values, beliefs, assumptions, and knowledge have been developed over time, are thought of as "truths," and are what guide people in their everyday lives. They are manifested in the taken-for-granted behaviors by which we function and often are manifested in opinions we hold. As Brookfield (1995) asserts, "we *are* our assumptions" (p. 2). For organizations to learn, however, individuals and teams must continually question, test, and validate these values, beliefs, assumptions, and knowledge in a public way. The exploration of individuals' mental models, knowledge structures, cognitive maps, schema, frameworks, and paradigms helps us understand the role of memory in learning and how future action may be predicted. Without examining what underlies our thinking, we are prone to continue operating in old ways, limiting the potential for learning and change (see Exhibit 3.4).

To understand individuals' underlying values, beliefs, assumptions, and knowledge with regard to an issue or problem, it is critical that organization members establish a climate of safety and trust. The goal is to understand why and how individuals believe the way they do about a particular issue. Specific activities can be used to help uncover members' values, beliefs, assumptions, and knowledge with respect to a particular issue facing the organization. For instance, group members can be asked to write their responses individually to each of the following questions:

- What are my roles/responsibilities with respect to this issue?
- How did I become involved in these roles/responsibilities?

EXHIBIT 3.4.

Benefits of Identifying and Clarifying Values, Beliefs, Assumptions, and Knowledge

▲ *Facilitates a common understanding of key terms and phrases so that language is less likely to be a barrier to effective communication and learning*

▲ *Brings to the surface motivations, opinions, and attitudes, which leads to greater understanding among team members*

▲ *Helps individual team members accept change and modify their thinking and behaviors*

▲ *Helps mediate potential conflicts among team members more quickly and effectively*

▲ *Confirms that prior experiences and attitudes affect individuals' behavior in the work environment*

- What experiences have I had with respect to this issue? Were they positive, negative, or neutral?
- What experiences in other settings have I had with respect to this issue? Were they positive, negative, or neutral?
- Have I had an experience with this issue where my expectations were not met? If so, why were they not met?
- How do I think this situation can be improved?
- Based on my answers to these questions, what underlying assumptions and values does my perspective on this issue reflect?
- In what ways might my values influence my position on this issue?

Sharing responses can help each group member more clearly see his or her value position as one among many in the organization. The following example illustrates what can happen when individuals' assumptions are not explored.

While conducting a multiyear evaluation of an educational reform effort, one of this book's authors learned that the four lead teachers, who were called a "team," had never discussed what it meant to be a team. From the outset, they simply assumed that they knew and agreed on what it meant to work as a team. During the school's experimental 3 years, the teachers met almost daily to discuss and resolve various issues that the school was experiencing, yet they found themselves in almost constant conflict about how these issues should be resolved. By the end of the school's third year, the teachers' relationships with one another had deteriorated to a point where they barely spoke to each other. What became clear to the evaluator was that the teachers were operating from very different mental models about teamwork and that this situation contributed to the group's inability to work together more effectively. For one teacher, being part of a team meant coming together only to decide on obviously significant issues. For another teacher, it meant daily meetings to decide on most of the school's operating policies and procedures by consensus. For another, it meant socializing with the staff before, during, and after school, and building a close-knit adult community. The effect of the teachers' different assumptions about teamwork was disastrous. At the end of the 3 years, the lead teachers all transferred to different schools and left the remaining teachers and staff feeling bewildered, frustrated, and angry. Once touted as a school of the future, the school now functions much like any other school. It would be wrong to conclude that the teachers' failure to define teamwork led to the school's failure at reform; however, it is likely that their inability to work as a team contributed to many of the problems the school faced in its first few years.

Identifying and clarifying individuals' values, beliefs, assumptions, and knowledge helps organization members appreciate why people talk and behave the way they do. In addition, knowing people's values, beliefs, assumptions, and knowledge helps them understand why an individual or group has trouble moving forward when there is disagreement about direction. As Ginger Juncker at Ford explained, "If I start talking and somebody says, 'oh, that's just a mental model,' we all know what we're talking about. It diffuses the situation. It takes the emotional side out of it" (GJ, Ford: 93). By acknowledging people's assumptions, others can understand without saying a perspective is right or wrong, or that they agree or disagree.

If a particular value or belief surfaces that is not desirable, individuals or groups can determine if the value or belief should be discarded or modified. At the same time, it is quite possible that certain values, beliefs, assumptions, and knowledge are validated as a result of the dialogue. In either case, what is most important is that organization members become conscious of existing values, beliefs, assumptions, and knowledge so that they may strive for a higher level of tolerance and understanding of each other. This learning process helps further the inquiry by encouraging team members to value and respect each individual's history, culture, and opinions.

The four learning processes described in this chapter are essential to enhancing individual, team, and organizational learning from evaluative inquiry. Dialogue is what facilitates a team's ability to reflect on individual values, beliefs, assumptions, and knowledge, as well as the asking of critical questions about the organizational issue being explored. In the next three chapters, we describe how one goes about focusing the inquiry, carrying out the inquiry, and applying learning from the inquiry, using each of the four learning processes.

NOTE

1. Readers familiar with Action Learning and Action Research forms of inquiry likely will be familiar with these learning processes. See Revans (1982), McGill and Beaty (1992), and Brooks and Watkins (1994) for resources on Action Learning; see Kemmis and McTaggart (1982), McTaggart (1991), and Cunningham (1993) for resources on Action Research.

CHAPTER 4

Focusing the Evaluative Inquiry

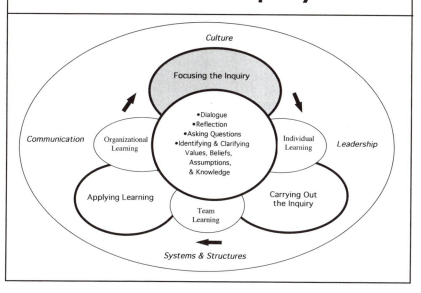

E very day, employees are faced with the need to make decisions and find solutions to new or persisting problems. These concerns might relate to a product's development that is behind schedule, customer complaints about service quality, a shrinking customer base, low employee morale, a training program's impact on employee performance, a teaching method's effect on student motivation and learning, the implementation of a particular organizational process or program, or how to best take advantage of new resources or opportunities. The approach organization members use to address these issues is what differentiates organizations that learn from their experiences from those that do not. In this chapter, we describe how a team focuses an inquiry through dialogue, reflection, asking questions, and identifying and clarifying values, beliefs, assumptions, and knowledge to

- define the evaluative issues.
- identify key stakeholders.
- determine a set of evaluative questions that will guide the inquiry.

This phase ensures that the issue of concern or interest is well articulated and agreed on by those who will likely use the evaluative inquiry's findings. As depicted in Figure 4.1, focusing the inquiry involves the continued definition and narrowing of the issue being studied.

INITIATING EVALUATIVE INQUIRY

Organizational life today provides employees with constant challenges that require solutions to problems, strategies to build on strengths, and creativity to imagine the future. Given this state of affairs, organizations are always facing new questions about how they should respond to continuing challenges and future action. One way to think about how issues arise in organizations is to explore how they begin. Consider the following kinds of "beginnings" and the questions they pose (Brinkerhoff, 1989):

- The *problem* beginning: A problem is noted somewhere in the organization that someone thinks is solvable. The questions being

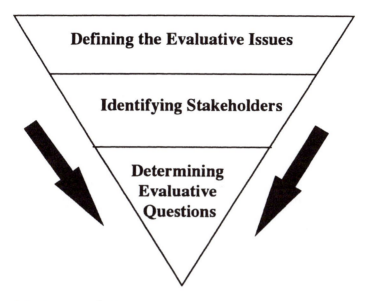

Figure 4.1. Focusing the Inquiry

asked include "What is the problem?" "Is it worth solving?" and "Why is it a problem?"

- The *change* beginning: Organizational change is imminent (e.g., hiring new employees; introducing new products or equipment; changes in legislation, rules, or regulations; offering new services; implementing new management approaches; reorganizing or reengineering). Problems are forecasted or projected rather than existing at the present time. Questions asked relative to this beginning include "What problems will the changes bring?" "Will the problems be worth solving?" and "What will help solve the problem?"

- The *opportunity* beginning: The organization is about to seize an opportunity that will change some aspect of organizational life. It might be thought of as a solution in search of a problem. The following questions apply to this type of beginning: "What might we do to maximize the organization's benefit from this opportu-

nity?" What are our options?" and "What are the potential consequences of one action over another?"

- The *strength* beginning: Rather than asking what is wrong, employees ask what is right for the purpose of building on the effective
  organizational processes, services, and systems already in place.
  For example, team members might ask "What are the strengths?"
  "How could the strength be extended to others?" "How could the
  strengths be further enhanced?" or "How can the strengths be
  maintained?"

- The *new direction* beginning: There are times when organizations
  seek opportunities to be proactive, to move beyond current problems or even strengths to new or greater levels of performance.
  This type of beginning focuses on assessing the opportunity's
  potential payoff to the organization. Questions here include "What
  is the current status?" "What new directions are available?" and
  "What changes would be most worthwhile?"

To show how these different kinds of beginnings help focus the
evaluative inquiry, one needs to look no further than the health care field
as an example of an industry undergoing unprecedented changes. Tran-
sitioning to a managed health care system is forcing health care providers to redefine their traditional practices. Instead of doctors waiting until
a patient comes in with a complaint, attention increasingly is being paid
to the areas of prevention, identification, and risk reduction. The
consolidation of doctors' practices into health maintenance organizations and other large management firms, however, requires that doctors
see more and more patients under strict guidelines about what costs will
and will not be covered by insurance companies. This shift limits the
time doctors can spend with patients and increases the perception that
the quality of health care is eroding, while putting money in the pockets
of corporate officers and shareholders. It is anticipated that by the year
2003, communities with more than 100,000 residents will be served by
only one to three health networks (Hamilton-KSA, 1996). The issue for
many health care providers is how to change a corporate culture of

control into one of collaboration that successfully integrates high quality with cost-effective services.

In describing what would happen if his hospital organization did not begin learning faster and better in today's market-driven economy, John Zondlo, an administrator at Presbyterian Hospital in Albuquerque, explained:

> We will lose market share. We will lose our ability to continue our mission of providing care to the people when they need it and where they need it. We just won't be able to compete with a declining pool of resources. So it will have operational and strategic implications. The environment is changing and it didn't always used to be that way. The health care environment used to be pretty stable during the days of cost-based reimbursement. It's not so anymore and things can change so quickly. I mean, the bill that's being debated today in the Senate on health care reform will have dramatic implications for us and 3 months ago no one was even sure that the bill was ever going to see the light of day. (JZ, Pres: 243)

This need to respond to impending changes in the health care industry is an example of a "change beginning." In other words, the organizations' leaders believe that in response to imminent changes, they will have to adapt their current ways of doing business if they want to stay viable for the long term. An organization's motivation to develop ongoing learning practices often results from "an urgency to act," or from a mismatch between what it wants to achieve and its actual outcomes (Argyris & Schon, 1978). Indeed, many of those we interviewed told us that their organizations' interest in becoming a learning organization was due to a perceived crisis and need to react quickly. Understanding the type of beginning that is the stimulus for learning allows organization members to more clearly frame and focus the inquiry effort.

Another way to conceptualize the beginnings of inquiry is to think about the reasons behind a perceived need to do something differently. For example, there might be interest in exploring the need for a particular program, or a desire to understand the effects or impact of an important process or program. Evaluative inquiry might be initiated because there is a need to understand how well a process or program is being implemented, or is reaching its intended audience(s). Having organization members consider the type of beginning and impetus for the inquiry is the first step in the focusing phase.

As discussed earlier in Chapter 2, the use of cross-functional, intact, and self-directed work teams of employees is becoming the primary method of solving problems and accomplishing work objectives in many organizations. The use of such teams is also central to implementing evaluative inquiry. Teams are the catalyst for action. A team that comes together to work on a departmental or organizational issue seeks to learn and apply their learning from evaluative inquiry processes. They first define the focus of their inquiry (this chapter), they then carry out the inquiry (Chapter 5), and finally they apply their learning to resolving or managing issues of concern (Chapter 6). Evaluative inquiry requires not only that teams learn about what actions to take as a result of inquiry but also that individuals learn about themselves and each other in the process. The ultimate goal of evaluative inquiry is to find common ground on which to act on organizational issues.

DEFINING THE EVALUATIVE ISSUE

When an issue has been identified, a departmental or organization-wide gathering might be called, inviting everyone who is interested in the topic to attend a meeting (e.g., see the Focused Dialogues strategy). After this initial meeting, it is likely that a core group of people will want to continue working on the issue. The resulting team could call itself a task force, an advisory team, a learning team, or whatever else it thought communicated its intended work. For example, a team at the Colorado Department of Education calls itself the 4-C team based on its goals: to coordinate, create, collaborate, and communicate.

When a team convenes, it begins a dialogue to explore the issue raised. Defining the issue begins with team members asking questions about

STRATEGY

Focused Dialogues

A focused dialogue starts with an invitation to up to 100 people in the organization who might be interested in the topic of the evaluative inquiry process. The invitation stresses that all who wish to come and join in the sharing and learning will be well received; participation is voluntary and is not mandated. The names of those who attend are not recorded. If people who are not invited attend, they too are welcomed. The goal is to have anyone who is even remotely interested in the topic feel welcomed. At the Electrical, Fuel, and Handling Division at Ford Motor Company, an invitation to 100 usually results in approximately 20-30 participants (KS, Ford: 28).

what they know, what they do not know, what they need to know, and why they need to know it relative to the topic being explored (see Patton [1997], Stecher & Davis [1987], and Worthen et al. [1997] for more on defining evaluative issues). The purpose is to engage in divergent thinking that includes gathering diverse points of view and analyzing the logic of a problem. Asking questions at this stage focuses the inquiry by concentrating on the issues and areas of concern that are deemed most important to the organization. It helps peel away the layers of ambiguity and vagueness that surround many issues we face in organizations. As team members ask more and more questions, such as "Tell me how this program works," and "How is it supposed to work?" the fundamental issue becomes more clearly illuminated. Let's use an artichoke as a metaphor. If you think about an artichoke's leaves, those on the outer layer contain just a bit of the flesh. As you labor away, peeling off leaf after leaf, always moving closer to the center, you find that the leaves contain more and more to eat. Finally, upon taking off all the leaves, you discover a protective layer of silklike threads. With just a bit more perseverance, you reach the heart—the core of the artichoke. Artichoke lovers everywhere know this is a just reward! Questioning raises team members' consciousness about the issue and

STRATEGY

Group Model Building

One approach to helping a team focus the inquiry is to have members divide up into groups of three to develop pictorial models that represent their thinking about the program or issue. Each group is provided with flip chart paper and several colored markers and is asked to collaboratively draw a picture of the issue facing the program, or groups might draw a logic model of the program itself. Once the models have been drawn on the flip chart paper, each group puts its model up on the wall. After discussing similarities and differences, the facilitator asks everyone what questions they have regarding the different models. Questions that address the underlying values, beliefs, assumptions, and knowledge of each model are asked, and implications stemming from the differences and similarities are discussed. These questions might include the following: What experiences have you had that led to this conceptualization? How would you describe the relationship between various components of the model? Where do you think the strengths or weaknesses are in the program as depicted in the model? From this dialogue, the entire team attempts to build a model that represents collective thinking about the issue being explored.

ultimately helps them focus on what is most important to learn—the heart of the matter. The strategy of Group Model Building provides a way of working through a team's perceptions of an issue.

While question asking helps to focus, it also provides team members an opportunity to see the larger context of the issue—it provides them with a more holistic picture of how the issue is related to other systems and practices. This zooming in and zooming out, much like a camera lens, enables the team to develop an understanding of, or a rationale for, the inquiry and provides a foundation on which all subsequent decisions about the inquiry effort will be based.

Questions team members might ask to begin defining the issue include:

4.1 What is the history or background of this problem/issue?

4.2 Have any previous inquiries been conducted regarding this topic? If yes, what were the results? How were the findings used?

4.3 Why is it important that we develop new insights into this problem/issue at this time?

4.4 What kinds of decisions would we like to make about the problem/issue?

4.5 What do we know about this problem/issue? What don't we know?

4.6 What organizational activities, procedures, or policies are part of the issue/problem?

4.7 What are the organizational variables that are affecting the context of the problem/issue?

4.8 What organizational politics are affecting the problem/issue?

4.9 What are our worst fears about this evaluative inquiry effort?

4.10 What are our hopes for what this evaluative inquiry effort will accomplish?

4.11 What is the purpose of the evaluative inquiry?

Answers to these questions reveal information about the program, how it fits within the organization, and individuals' values, beliefs, assumptions, and knowledge about the program.

Team members must be provided opportunities to reflect on their understanding and experiences relative to the emerging focus of the inquiry. When they have an opportunity to share their reflections, they can better understand, and be more honest about, the origins and consequences of their own thinking and behavior. One way to do this is by using a strategy called Open Space Technology, which uncovers a large group's interests and concerns about a topic being explored.

Consider for example, a team that is discussing what to do about customers' complaints regarding the organization's "technology hot line." Callers are saying that the technicians are not helpful and that some even seem angry that they are calling. After members reflect both individually and as a team, one team member says that she believes customers just do not bother to read the technical documentation or directions—mostly because they are lazy. She is upset that people do not understand even the simplest procedures and believes they would have no problem if only they read the material. After some reflection and

STRATEGY

Open Space Technology

In 1983, Harrison Owen began working with the Open Space Technology concept. Based on a belief that the "circle is the fundamental geometry of open human communication" (1992, p. 5), where all people are face to face and equal, he has used the following process all over the world as a means to create a mechanism for dialogue. Open Space Technology not only creates opportunities for brainstorming topics or issues of concern but also encourages open dialogue and ultimately action on the questions raised. In this way, it facilitates evaluative inquiry in general and focusing the inquiry phase in particular. Open Space Technology is particularly effective where groups of diverse people have to deal with complex, and potentially conflicting issues and where the focus is on real business. The following guidelines are excerpted from Owen's book *Open Space Technology: A User's Guide* (1992).

- Anyone who cares about the general topic is invited to attend (attendance must be voluntary). Anywhere from 5 to 500 can participate. At least 1 full day is needed—a maximum of 3 is recommended.

- The process requires a large room where all participants can sit in a circle or two or three concentric circles. One wall of the room must be free and unobstructed. This wall will be called the Community Bulletin Board, where people will be putting up pieces of paper with their areas of interest. Break-out rooms will be necessary for groups of people to meet.

- You will need masking tape (five rolls per 100 participants), washable ink markers (50 per 100 participants), and flip charts (one per break-out room plus five additional pads per 100 participants). These numbers are estimates only.

- Create a safe and comfortable environment. Post and explain the following rules:
  1. Show up
  2. Be present
  3. Tell the truth
  4. Let it all go

STRATEGY

Open Space Technology (continued)

- State the theme, purpose, and objective of the day.
- Describe the process. You might say something like this:

> I am going to ask each one of you who cares to, and nobody has to—to identify some issue or opportunity related to our theme, for which you have genuine passion, and for which you will take real responsibility. Don't just consider good ideas that somebody else might do, or be interested in. Think of powerful ideas that really grab you to the point that you will take personal responsibility to make sure that something gets done. If nothing occurs to you, that is OK, and if you have more than one issue or opportunity, that is fine too. Once you have your issue or opportunity in mind, come out into the center of the circle, and grab a piece of paper and a magic marker. Write down a short title and sign your name. Then stand in front of the group and say, "My issue is—my name is." After you have announced your theme, take your piece of paper and tape it on that blank wall (pp. 60-61).

- The blank wall (Community Bulletin Board) can be made so that times and break-out rooms are designated, and the themes can be posted in one of the time slots on the board. This will help participants see how the day is being constructed and know where to meet their group. You may decide that each time slot should be for 1 or 2 hours.
- Once all the themes are on the Community Bulletin Board, participants go up to the board and sign their names in as many of the time slots/themes as they wish.
- Participants are told to go forth and see what happens.
- At the end of each session, participants return to the Village Marketplace and share their learning or negotiate changes to the next group of sessions. Participants can change their minds about the groups they will be joining, sessions can be combined, or conflicts can be worked out.
- The role of the facilitator is to become invisible.

(continued on next page)

STRATEGY

Open Space Technology (continued)

Additional principles:

- Whoever comes are the right people.
- Whatever happens is the only thing that could have.
- Whenever it starts is the right time.
- When it is over it is over.
- Enact the Law of Two Feet—if participants feel their time would be better spent somewhere else, they can and should leave.
- Encourage Butterflies and Bumblebees—Butterflies often do not go to any groups and seek to be alone. Sometimes others will join them and conversation ensues; other times, they contribute nothing. Bumblebees, on the other hand, flit from one group to another, only touching down briefly in each group they visit. "They pollinate and cross pollinate" (p. 73) and often leave rich and thought-provoking ideas in the groups they have visited.

SOURCE: Adapted from *Open Space Technology: A User's Guide*, Owen, © 1992 by Abbott Publishing.

talking with other team members, she acknowledges that her curtness with customers may be associated with her "laziness" assumption. She realizes that her assumption is based on a judgment she has made about laziness that influences her behavior with customers. She begins to question this assumption, and with the help of team members she is able to consider alternative reasons why callers may have such questions. These new insights allow her to think more realistically about customer service issues.

A method for helping teams reflect at this stage of the focusing phase is described in the Critical Incidents strategy. Here team members reflect on their previous experiences with the program or process being studied.

STRATEGY

Critical Incidents

The critical incident method is an effective way of helping people reflect on their experiences and recall memorable or significant events regarding an issue or topic. The exercise involves asking team members a number of questions that they respond to either in writing or orally (Brookfield, 1995; Cranton, 1994; Preskill, 1997). For example, if a team was interested in understanding how well a new personal career development planning process was working in an organization, it might be asked to respond to the following questions:

1. Can you think of a time when your development plan helped you see your career in a new light? What was it about the plan that made you feel this way?

2. Can you think of a time when you felt the development plan got in the way of your career planning? What happened here?

3. What action has someone in the organization taken to help you implement your development plan?

4. What have you found most puzzling or confusing about using your development plan?

5. What has surprised you the most about developing and using this plan?

After team members reflect on these questions individually, they can be discussed as a large group, or members can share their responses in pairs or triads in which each person questions the others about the underlying assumptions and beliefs of their responses. Team members should be able to ask indirect questions of each other—"Why did you say this?" and "What led you to describe it this way?"

This strategy facilitates individuals' ability to recall an experience and to replay it in their mind, or to remember the feelings associated with the experience. The exercise clarifies individuals' underlying values, beliefs, assumptions, and knowledge relative to the subject of the inquiry.

To illustrate the benefits of revealing values, beliefs, assumptions, and knowledge, Beth Shober from the Colorado Department of Education told us that in her area of prevention initiatives, team members generally agree that what they are doing is important to society. When it comes to the words "prevention" and "comprehensive health," however, it is likely that individuals' definitions are vastly different from one another. She explained that having different definitions is not inherently "bad," but she did admit that sending mixed messages, based on different assumptions, to the public is not a good idea (BS, CDE: 292). The process of identifying and clarifying members' values, beliefs, assumptions, and knowledge therefore helps team members develop a richer conception of the issue and how they might approach further phases of the inquiry process.

As team members learn about (a) each person's experiences with the issue, (b) the assumptions they have made about the purpose and content of the issue, (c) what they believe about the issue, and (d) the values that guide their behaviors and attitudes regarding the issue, they develop a greater appreciation for each other. For example, suppose a group of trainers came together to determine which training method(s) would be most effective for developing managers' coaching skills. One trainer, who firmly believes in the lecture method, refuses to include experiential activities, claiming they are "fluff" and a "waste of time." In spite of other team members' attempts to convince her of the value of other instructional approaches, she remains unwavering in her belief about the lecture method. By using a "Ladder of Inference" tool (Senge et al., 1994, p. 243), we can examine how her assumptions might be guiding her thinking. We can observe the sequence of her thinking process by following the logic statements of her argument. The reasoning behind each statement is provided in parentheses.

▲ I prefer the lecture of method of instruction because the learners have much to learn and this method allows for a lot of content to be presented. (This represents data based on my observations and experiences.)

▲ The majority of people are used to the lecture method because most of our education has been delivered this way, and we seem to have learned a lot. (I have selected some details from what I have observed; I have experienced group activities but have not been drawn to using such methods.)

▲ The learners seem to be listening when I talk. (I believe that when people look at you while you are talking, they must be listening; I have added my own cultural and personal meanings.)

▲ Because they seem to be listening, I am sure they are learning a lot. (Based on my observations and assumptions so far, I am convinced that they are learning; I have added meaning to my assumptions.)

▲ If they learn a lot, they will perform better on their jobs. (Now I can conclude that my training will be effective.)

▲ Improving job performance is what my job is all about. Through my training of employees, I add value to this organization. (This represents my belief about what is important to the organization.)

▲ I will continue using the lecture method because it works. (I am taking actions based on my beliefs.)

Without questioning her values and judgments, this person is locked into a pattern of reasoning that perpetuates misperceptions about how people learn. Because her assumptions have gone unchallenged, her values and beliefs are reinforced every time she teaches. Each step of the way, her values and assumptions about what is important guide her reasoning. Not until someone questions these specific assumptions will she begin to view the situation differently.

Exploring the sequence of inferences is particularly useful in that it allows one's assumptions, or different expectations, to become more visible to others. Although people might not agree with the statements being made, this process significantly helps clarify misunderstandings between individuals and enables them to ask questions relative to each stage of thinking. At the same time, understanding each other does not necessarily mean agreeing with each other. Although team members might not agree with the trainer's logic, they can at least see what is motivating her statements and actions. From there, they can begin to offer alternatives based on the inferences she has made. Another example of the usefulness of understanding an individual's assumptions is explained by Ginger Juncker, a production/supplier team leader at Ford:

> I can perfectly well understand what you're saying and what you mean, but disagree. And so that's where when we say "mental model"; it allows us to talk and understand one another in a terminology that does not mean agreeing. Because if you say mental models, it doesn't mean that you're right. All I'm saying is that you have an opinion and let's talk about it. (GJ, Ford: 96)

By uncovering and sharing team members' values, beliefs, assumptions, and knowledge, individuals continually clarify how they perceive the various dimensions of the issue being explored (see the Using Questions to Explore Values, Beliefs, Assumptions, and Knowledge strategy). This process often reveals how individual team members carry around different definitions of organizational success and expected outcomes. Furthermore, as team members begin to understand each other's values, beliefs, assumptions, and knowledge regarding an issue, they may become more willing and able to modify their own thinking and behaviors.

IDENTIFYING STAKEHOLDERS

Once team members clearly understand why the evaluative inquiry effort is worthy of further attention, they must identify those individuals and groups who are interested in the topic and are intended users of the evaluative inquiry's process and outcomes (also see Patton, 1997; Posavac & Carey, 1997). Program staff, administrators, policymakers, students, clients, customers, managers, supervisors, parents—all may have an interest in being or need to be part of the inquiry effort or be apprised of the inquiry's findings. Some of these people already will be part of the team; however, it is quite likely that there are many other stakeholders, both internal and external to the organization, who would benefit from participating in the evaluative

STRATEGY

Using Questions to Explore Values, Beliefs, Assumptions, and Knowledge in the Focusing Phase

To help team members explore their values, beliefs, assumptions, and knowledge during the focusing stage, the facilitator might ask each team member to do the following in relation to the issue being discussed:

- Explain the information you have used to develop this opinion.
- Explain the context of your point of view and how you think your perspective might affect others.
- Give examples of what led you to this assumption or belief.

As individuals respond to the above, team members may ask clarifying questions such as:

- How does it affect how you make decisions?
- Have you considered . . . ?
- If I understand you correctly, you are saying that . . .
- What leads you to conclude that?
- What do you mean?
- What is the significance of that?
- Can you help me understand your thinking here?

Individuals' responses to these questions should help team members understand each other's perceptions about the inquiry topic, thus allowing them to address the issue more fully, and at a deeper level.

SOURCE: Adapted from *The Fifth Discipline Fieldbook*, Senge et al. (pp. 256-285), © 1994 by Doubleday.

inquiry effort at some level. It is important to involve as many stakeholders as possible in understanding the inquiry's purpose and findings.

A team might begin identifying stakeholders by asking members to explain why they are interested in participating in the evaluative inquiry effort, what they hope to learn, and how they plan to use the findings.

For stakeholders not involved in the inquiry, efforts should be made to ask them what they see as their most important information needs relative to the issue being explored. Identifying stakeholders involves reflection about who the stakeholders might be, why they are stakeholders, and what role they should play in the inquiry process. When teams come together, they often think that only a few individuals or groups are stakeholders—usually those closest to the program being studied. As team members reflect on the larger context of the object being evaluated, they find that indeed, there are many more potential stakeholders. Some questions to ask at this stage of the focusing phase include

4.12 What individuals or groups were mentioned as we worked to define the issues for this inquiry? What is their involvement with the problem/issue?

4.13 Why do we believe that each of these individuals or groups is a stakeholder?

4.14 How might each of these individuals or groups be affected by the outcomes of this inquiry?

4.15 Which individuals or groups might use the findings for policy-making decisions?

4.16 Which individuals or groups might use the findings for making operational decisions?

4.17 Which individuals or groups might be interested in the findings but are not in a decision-making position relative to the subject of the inquiry?

4.18 Who has a "right to know" about the inquiry's results?

4.19 Which of these individuals or groups should be involved in the process of the inquiry but are not currently on the inquiry team?

Through reflection and dialogue, a team can focus on its underlying beliefs about who needs to know the results and why. It would not be surprising to find that team members have different notions of who is and who is not a stakeholder. The resulting negotiations lead to a more inclusive and diverse set of stakeholders and an increased understanding of the information needs of various individuals and groups.

DETERMINING EVALUATIVE QUESTIONS

Once the issue is clearly defined and the stakeholders are identified and agreed upon by team members, the last step of the focusing phase is the development of a set of evaluative questions that form the boundaries and parameters of the inquiry effort (see also Stake, 1995, and Worthen et al., 1997). These broadly worded, typically open-ended questions further define the topic and, just as important, guide future decisions about what methods of data collection should be used (see Chapter 5). A common mistake made in many evaluative inquiry projects is that a team jumps to selecting a method of data collection without first considering the questions the inquiry is to address. This approach "puts the cart before the horse." Until we know what the evaluative questions are, we cannot possibly know what data collection methods will most appropriately address the topic of the evaluative inquiry. The danger in choosing methods before developing evaluative questions is that the team may end up collecting a lot of information that in the end is not useful; that is, information that was not critical to the team's decision-making and learning needs.

From the previous dialogue on defining the issue and identifying stakeholders, the team should have begun to generate questions it wants the inquiry to address. It may have kept track of these questions on flip chart paper, or a team member might have documented these in her notes. Most likely, the questions posed in the early stages of the focusing phase are quite diverse; some are very specific and others are very broad. This is the time, however, to pay particular attention to refining the purpose of the evaluative inquiry and the questions it will seek to answer. To develop the evaluative questions, team members might ask:

4.20 What questions should the inquiry seek to answer?

4.21 Why are these evaluative questions important?

4.22 What must we know now, and what can we wait to know?

4.23 Which are the most critical questions?

4.24 What are the consequences if we do not answer these questions soon?

4.25 What do we hope will happen by answering these questions?

4.26 What do we think will happen if the answers to these questions are not in line with what certain stakeholders believe is true?

Often, settling on a set of questions requires intense negotiation with stakeholders (those on and off the team). It should be remembered, however, that in the spirit of organizational learning, not all questions must be answered through this one inquiry effort. The team may think numerous questions are important, but the team does not have enough time or resources to address them all. At this point, it is important to discuss what will happen with the questions that will not be addressed. When evaluative inquiry is interwoven into organizational systems and processes, efforts will be made to interest others in taking on the questions that cannot be addressed at this time, or the original team might decide to consider these other questions as part of an additional inquiry effort. Because evaluative inquiry is an ongoing process and not an event that happens once in a while, team members know that eventually all questions raised will be addressed.

The number of questions that the team arrives at will vary significantly from project to project; however, it should be clear that the more questions the team poses, the more comprehensive the evaluative inquiry will be. The evaluative questions the team agrees upon answering should be those that some form of inquiry can address: In other words, the questions are answerable through the collection, analysis, and interpretation of data.

As with the other steps in the focusing phase, it is difficult to come to agreement and understanding about the evaluative questions without considering why certain things are important to some individuals and not to others. The process of developing evaluative questions encourages team members to articulate why they think a certain question is important and relevant to the inquiry effort. Their assumptions and opinions underlying their support of particular questions should be explored. This step facilitates the negotiation of the final set of evaluative questions by enabling all team members to understand the motivations behind individuals' information needs. The continual exploration of team members' values, beliefs, assumptions, and knowledge enables organi-

EXHIBIT 4.1.

Benefits of Focusing the Inquiry

▲ *Allows team members to view a specific problem or issue within the larger context of the organization*

▲ *Clarifies the relationship between program goals, design, and intended outcomes*

▲ *Enables competing expectations of the program to be explored and understood*

▲ *Highlights potential barriers or obstacles to further evaluative inquiry processes*

▲ *Clarifies intended users and intended uses of evaluative inquiry outcomes*

▲ *Identifies potential misuses of evaluative inquiry processes*

▲ *Increases the likelihood that the information needs of diverse groups of individuals (stakeholders) will be considered and included in the evaluative inquiry process, which leads to an enhanced use of findings*

▲ *Increases the likelihood that meaningful and useable data will be obtained in carrying out the inquiry phase*

▲ *Identifies questions that may provide insights into other issues that would benefit from additional inquiry*

▲ *Ensures that the most significant questions will be addressed in the evaluative inquiry process*

zation members to develop deeper insights into how what people think and experience influence the culture and direction of the organization.

By the end of the focusing phase, a team will have developed a set of critical questions they are interested in and committed to answering through the remaining evaluative inquiry phases (see Exhibit 4.1). The team will have identified individuals and groups who will be

interested in the process and outcomes of the inquiry, and it will have acquired a larger perspective of the issue's context. In addition, members should feel a sense of common purpose and have learned more about critical organizational issues and about themselves and each other as well. They will be clear about what they have learned so far and what they still need to learn.

ILLUSTRATIVE CASE—FOCUSING THE INQUIRY

To help readers further understand how the four learning processes facilitate the three phases of evaluative inquiry, we offer the following case example to clarify and articulate these processes. We begin the case in this chapter and continue it through the *carrying out the inquiry* and *applying learning* phases (Chapters 5 and 6).

Some Background

A local nonprofit service organization is concerned about the decreasing number of people using one of its program's services. The program was begun several years ago in an effort to provide information and support to women with breast cancer. Designed as a volunteer visitation program, it focuses on meeting the emotional, physical, and cosmetic needs related to breast cancer and its treatment. It is a one-on-one visitation program that provides educational literature, exercise equipment, and a list of resources to clients. Women who are 1-year post surgery, are not undergoing any treatment, and have the approval of their physician are invited to be volunteers in the program, and whenever possible, a match between the cancer patient and the volunteer is made to facilitate understanding and communication. For many years, it was the only program available to women who had been diagnosed with breast cancer. Recent trends, however, have alerted several staff members to issues they believe are important to address. They believe that increased competition from other service providers and a lack of effective marketing to health care providers and the community are contributing to a decline in referrals to the program.

The program's director has decided that the issue (a problem beginning) should be addressed through an evaluative inquiry process. An external evaluation consultant was hired as a facilitator because few staff members have experience conducting an inquiry process. With the help and support of the director, a group of people involved in the program were invited to participate in the project. This six-member team, consisting of program staff and volunteers, became known as the Evaluative Inquiry Team. The team first came together to begin the *focusing the inquiry* phase. The facilitator began by asking team members to introduce themselves, describing their experiences with the program, the history of the program, and any areas of concern they had about the program.

The facilitator then asked what they "believed to be true" about the program. She asked them to reflect by themselves for 5 minutes on their experiences with and perceptions about the program, and to jot down any thoughts they had on a pad of paper. At the end of the 5 minutes, she engaged the group in a dialogue about their beliefs and experiences. During this time she, as well as the team members, asked individuals how they came to hold these views. For example, she asked:

▲ What do you think the purpose of this program is? Why does it exist?

▲ What would happen if the program ceased to exist?

▲ Why is this program important to you?

▲ How do you think this program has affected the lives of its clients?

▲ Has a friend or anyone in your family used the program's services? If yes, what effect did the program have on your friend and/or family member?

▲ What do you think are the biggest challenges facing the delivery of this service?

▲ What other programs or services are you also involved in regarding this disease? How has your involvement in these programs or services affected your perception of this program?

▲ What do you think might be true about the program, but you have no data to support?

From this dialogue, the team members began to see that although they all wanted the program to continue and succeed, they had varied reasons why they thought referrals were declining. Furthermore, they learned that some team members had expectations for the program that were not explicitly stated in the program's goals. The dialogue process revealed team members' different experiences with the program and how these experiences shaped their beliefs and assumptions about the program's impact on its clients.

The inquiry facilitator then asked them to write down, on sticky notes, two or three questions they had about the program. These questions, she explained, could relate to the program's effectiveness, resources, implementation, administration, materials, customer satisfaction, or any other aspect of the program they were curious or concerned about. As they finished writing their questions, they were asked to place their sticky notes next to other similar questions on pieces of flip chart paper. When everyone was finished, the facilitator read each question and the team developed a label that described the questions in that grouping. If a question no longer fit with the topic, it was placed on hold until another category emerged that encompassed the thought. The result of this process was six categories, with three to six questions per category.

The focusing process then shifted to a period of negotiation among team members. Here they had to decide where they wanted to go with the evaluative inquiry effort. The facilitator guided this process by asking questions about what was important to them, what information was most critical to them in the short term, what aspects of the program could they most likely affect, and how they might address some of the other questions in a future inquiry effort. Again, after a period of some reflection, the team went back to the questions originally written on sticky notes and prioritized each category of questions. The members finally agreed to focus the inquiry on seven evaluative questions. The questions that fell to the bottom of the list were not discarded; instead, the team suggested that another team might come together to address these larger organizational questions at a later time.

Throughout this dialogue, various individuals' names were raised as those who would be most interested in the evaluative inquiry's process as well as its findings. The team made a list of stakeholders that included program staff, clients served, volunteers, and health care providers in the area. As each individual or group was mentioned, the team reflected on why these people would be interested and what their information needs might be, along with discussing the values, beliefs, assumptions, and knowledge on which they made these determinations.

The outcome of the focusing process was not only the evaluative questions that would be addressed but also (a) the team's understanding of how each member experienced the program and (b) what values, beliefs, assumptions, and knowledge were guiding daily interactions with the program and its clients. Throughout the process, team members often admitted they had not known something about the program that another team member had shared. Several times, individuals said they thought they were the only ones who had perceived the situation in a particular way. At times, team members expressed surprise when learning something about a team member that they did not know before and were happy to know.

The *focusing the inquiry* phase resulted in the following purpose statement, list of stakeholders, and evaluative questions.

Purpose

The purpose of this inquiry is to determine the extent to which the program is meeting the needs of women it is serving and to explore ways in which the program can be improved.

Stakeholders (Intended Users of the Evaluative Inquiry's Process and Findings)

- Program staff and volunteers
- Clients
- Health care providers

Evaluative Questions

1. To what extent is the program meeting the educational and emotional needs of the women it serves?

2. How satisfied are women with the program?

3. What changes have women made in their lifestyles as a result of their involvement in the program?

4. What aspects of the program have women found to be most useful or helpful in their recovery? Not useful?

5. In what ways might the program make its services more visible to women?

6. How do women learn about the program?

7. How aware are health care providers about the services of the program?

Now that they were clear about the purpose of the inquiry effort, had identified stakeholders, and had developed a set of questions that needed answering, they were ready to carry out the inquiry. This case example is continued at the conclusion of Chapter 5.

CHAPTER **5**

Carrying Out
the Inquiry

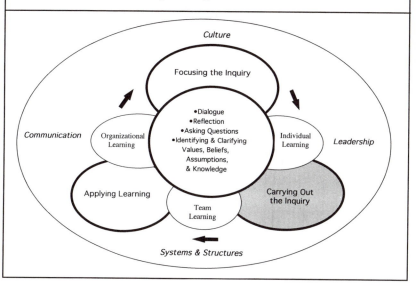

O nce a team has focused the object of its inquiry and developed specific evaluative questions (as explained in Chapter 4), it most likely will see the need to gather data to address these questions. In this chapter, we describe how a team establishes a means for collecting, analyzing, and interpreting data, and communicating and reporting the inquiry's process and findings. The commitment to gathering data is central to evaluative inquiry. As team members consider the data collected in the light of their own values, beliefs, assumptions, and knowledge, and what they have learned from and about each other, they create new understandings about the issue being explored—further nourishing individual, team, and organizational learning.

The work of evaluative inquiry in this phase most closely resembles traditional evaluation or action research efforts—with the crucial enhancement being that the four learning processes of dialogue, reflection, asking questions, and identifying and clarifying values, beliefs, assumptions, and knowledge are inextricably intertwined throughout the design, data collection, analysis and interpretation, and communicating and reporting activities. The key task at this time is to clearly link the information needs of the stakeholders to the evaluative questions and the kinds of data that will best answer those questions. Although an evaluation consultant might facilitate this process, it is important that practitioners learn inquiry skills as well so that these tools and processes can be used readily and shared within the organization for future inquiry efforts. An evaluation consultant, one who may have developed a long-term relationship with the organization, can facilitate training or provide technical assistance on how to design, collect, analyze, and interpret data.

When most people think of collecting data or conducting an evaluation, they often think of it as being a massive effort requiring months of time and considerable resources. Although some inquiries will involve substantial effort, the collection, analysis, and interpretation of data need not be a terribly cumbersome and complex task. What is most important is that the team establishes a method for determining the type and amount of data needed to produce sufficient, trustworthy, useable information. Data quality is only as good as the methods used for collection and analysis. For example, using a generic post-course survey to evaluate trainees' reactions to a training program that has not been tailored to the most pressing evaluative questions of the trainers and the organization likely will not provide useful information. When we collect data that do not adequately address our questions about a problem or issue, it is both a waste of resources and unfair to those who are providing the data. The systematic, planned, and rigorous collection and documentation of data is what distinguishes true evaluative inquiry from anecdotal, unplanned, and less credible forms of data collection.

What follows in this chapter is not meant to provide basic instruction in traditional program evaluation activities (see note 1, Introduction) but rather to build on practitioners' existing knowledge by illustrating how the four learning processes described in Chapter 3 can be used in conjunction with conventional evaluation and applied research activities within organizations. The chapter is organized according to two main efforts: *designing the inquiry* and *implementing inquiry activities*. Each of these sections covers the collection, analysis, and interpretation of data, and communicating and reporting of the inquiry's processes and findings. Additionally, the first section, on designing the inquiry, provides examples of planning formats for data collection and communicating and reporting. As will be shown, the different learning processes are interwoven throughout this phase of the evaluative inquiry.

DESIGNING THE INQUIRY

The *carrying out the inquiry* phase begins with its design—that is, the process of choosing and detailing the most appropriate approach for collecting, analyzing, and interpreting data. The approach taken might involve any of the following means for obtaining data:

- A specific one-time inquiry or study
- An information system that will collect and maintain data on an ongoing basis
- A means for utilizing data already available through an existing information system

The choice among these options typically depends on two factors: (a) the extent to which data may be needed and/or available on an ongoing versus a one-time basis, and (b) what data collection or management information systems already exist within the organization. For example, a school district might decide to assess the status of a change in its high school curriculum that eliminates ability-level courses and focuses on differentiated instruction within classrooms. This kind of inquiry would be conducted as a one-time study because its purpose is to assess circumstances at the present time, and the data collection instruments would contain questions relevant to recent and current events.

As another example, a nonprofit organization experiencing increased demands for documentation of results might see the need to develop data collection and reporting systems that routinely measure program inputs, outputs, and intermediate and long-term outcomes (see Newcomer, 1997). Here, because the organization needs to review results over time and periodically report them, the best approach would most likely be to develop an information system that will collect and maintain data on an ongoing basis.

Finally, an organization might decide to make better use of an existing information system. Sometimes such systems are maintained within organizations but are underutilized for a variety of reasons (see Chapter 7 for more on communication within organizations). At this point, the inquiry team would be concerned with determining how well available data will answer the evaluative inquiry questions, and in what ways the existing system might need to be modified or used differently to carry out the inquiry effectively.

Whichever approach is taken, the design of the inquiry is by far the most significant element for carrying it out successfully. Mere enthusiasm about proceeding with the inquiry, as well as a pressing need for the information it will provide, may create an impetus to initiate data collection activities too promptly once specific evaluative inquiry questions have been developed. Inquiry teams are well advised to resist this temptation. Careful planning and anticipation of resources needed is especially important if the inquiry will be carried out by those in the organization. These individuals likely will be taking on their role in the evaluative inquiry as an add-on to an already full roster of responsibilities. Design decisions may be made too quickly based on at least four factors:

- Preferred methods of those experienced in data collection and analysis activities
- Prior experiences of team members with data collection and analysis activities
- Unexamined notions, perceptions, or prior knowledge about the organization's culture
- Perceived methodological, time, or other logistical constraints

During the design stage, these factors must be given careful scrutiny to arrive at the most relevant, contextually sensitive, and productive, yet efficient, means for *carrying out the inquiry*. In particular, it is during the design stage that the inquiry team should rekindle the spirit of openness and exploration that was present in the *focusing the inquiry* phase. The strategy for Developing a Database for Organizational Learning illustrates the significant level of effort, involving all members of an organization, required to design a means for data collection that best addresses the organization's evaluative questions.

Engaging in evaluative inquiry involves a continuous process of judgments and decisions about how to conduct the inquiry. These judgments typically result from what is essentially a process of asking questions. When judgments are made, however, they usually are based on an individual's or team's underlying values, beliefs, assumptions, and knowledge. It is important that these influences be uncovered and examined in the process of making decisions about how to collect, analyze, and interpret data. Although certain values, beliefs, assumptions, and knowledge may be accurate and/or appropriate in a given situation, it is important that they be checked so that other possibilities can be considered. During the design stage, all aspects of the inquiry (data collection, analysis and interpretation, communicating and reporting) must be planned. The inquiry design should begin with preliminary considerations addressing both team members' and the organization's prior experiences with data collection activities. A process of asking questions, reflection, and dialogue typically is in order. The inquiry team can use the following set of questions to better understand how their previous inquiry experiences might affect the present inquiry:

STRATEGY

Developing a Database
for Organizational Learning

Through an effort to address long-standing concerns about staff workload, efficiency, and effectiveness, a large U.S.-based management consulting firm recognized that the organization was not garnering the benefit of its collective experience over time and across its many consulting projects. Although the firm was financially successful, many consultants had observed that they rarely had a chance to fully integrate what they had learned from one project before moving on to the next one. Nor did they have much time to communicate with others in the firm what they were doing and learning in the course of their work. At the same time, the firm also recognized that although basic information about projects was maintained in paper files and on a database, it was not being maintained consistently—nor did it reflect all the descriptive information necessary to summarize projects for periodic internal reports to the firm's management. The firm identified three major questions it used to focus an ongoing inquiry effort:

1. What are individual consultants and work teams learning about interactions with clients?
2. How can these lessons be captured and used across the firm?
3. What basic, descriptive information does the firm need about projects for internal reporting and tracking?

To address these questions, the firm identified the need for an organizational learning system but also recognized that it did not have the technical expertise or personnel time to develop and implement the system. External consultants who could provide the necessary analytical, facilitation, and technical skills were hired to work in close collaboration with the firm's staff. The external consultants worked with a cross-functional Organizational Learning Advisory Team to develop a two-phased approach:

- Analyze the firm's information and learning needs/requirements.
- Develop a plan for an organizational learning system that meets these requirements.

STRATEGY

Developing a Database
for Organizational Learning (continued)

The following paragraphs describe how each phase was carried out and show the iterative and collaborative tack taken. Although the purpose of the work was to help the firm become a learning organization, the work itself was undertaken using solid organizational learning principles.

Phase 1, the analysis of the firm's information and learning needs/requirements, resulted in two products: (a) graphic illustrations detailing the firm's operations, including the flow of formal and informal operations; and (b) specific objectives for the organizational learning system based on identified information and learning needs/requirements. The consultants conducted individual interviews with the firm's staff in two rounds to learn (a) defining characteristics of the firm's organizational context and culture, (b) how the firm operates in general as well as specific details of project management and work team practices, (c) the nature and course of formal and informal information flow in these practices, and (d) what information and learning needs/ requirements staff have. The first round was with 18 key informants from across all departments. To obtain further detail about various processes and procedures, the second round of 15 interviews was with project staff from different work teams.

From the analysis of these interview data, drafts of (a) the graphic illustration of the firm's operations and information flow and (b) specific objectives for the organizational learning system were developed. The consultants presented these drafts to all employees of the firm (in groups of 10 to 15) for review, additional input, discussion, and modification. To maximize the results of these dialogues, some groups were composed of within-department staff and others were composed of across-department staff. During the dialogues, the consultants worked with the staff to resolve discrepancies and variances in perceptions about how the firm operated and what its information and learning needs/requirements were. In fact, it was clear to all present that the dialogues resulted in new understandings that would not otherwise have been possible. The consultants pooled the results of all dialogues and revised the products of the first phase accordingly. These products were then presented to the Organizational Learning Advisory Group for further review, discussion, and final approval.

(continued on next page)

STRATEGY

Developing a Database
for Organizational Learning (continued)

Phase 2, development of an implementation plan for the organizational learning system, resulted in two products: (a) functional specifications for the computer program (database) that supports the system, and (b) detailed descriptions of the manual (i.e., noncomputerized) aspects of the system. The functional specifications provided a complete technical description of the desired external behavior of the computer program to be built; that is, the specifications provided graphic and verbal descriptions of what the database software would do to support the organizational learning system. Details of the noncomputerized aspects of the system included (a) a written description of the manual systems of maintaining and tracking information, (b) staff activities to glean "best practices" and "lessons learned" (e.g., frequency and topics of meetings/discussions, etc.), and (c) interactions between the database and manual aspects of the organizational learning system.

Based on the products of Phase 1, drafts of the products just described for Phase 2 were developed. At the same time, the external consultants began reviewing commercial off-the-shelf database programs that might meet the firm's needs. Also, to flesh out the details of the plan and identify various software solutions, the external consultants identified the need for a deeper level of more specific information about the firm's operations. They conducted a third round of interviews with selected staff and, based on this input, refined details of the plan. It was then presented to all staff, in the same fashion used in Phase 1—iterative rounds of review, additional input, discussion, and modification. A final version of the plan was presented to the Organizational Learning Advisory Group for review and approval.

5.1 What kinds of data does the organization typically respond to? What does it ignore?

5.2 To what extent was the type of data from previous studies considered credible by the organization?

5.3 What are the preferred methods of those responsible for carrying out the data collection and analysis activities for the present inquiry?

5.4 What political issues related to the use of different data collection methods have surfaced in the past?

5.5 How might the answers to any of these questions influence decisions about the present inquiry?

Answers to the above questions may identify a wide variety of contextual or even political issues that could affect how specific data collection activities are designed and implemented. For example, a concern that other organizational members will be threatened by collecting data on outcomes related to their work might be addressed by involving them in this phase of the evaluative inquiry and/or taking special care to communicate with others the intent and purpose of data collection activities.

METHODS AND PROCEDURES
FOR DATA COLLECTION

As the team begins to think about different data collection methods and procedures, it is important to understand that data may be of two types: *quantitative* (numbers, such as percentages or mean scores from Likert-type survey items or test questions) or *qualitative* (represented in the form of words or pictures as would be gathered from interviews, observations, photographs, videotapes, and drawings). Quantitative data tell us how much, how often, and how many; qualitative data inform us of the how, what, and why of what we are studying. Because all data collection methods have inherent weaknesses and provide limited insights, it is best to consider the collection of both qualitative and quantitative data through more than one method. (See Greene and Caracelli [1997] and Mertens [1997] for in-depth treatments of using qualitative and quantitative methods in evaluation studies.)

As the team considers different data collection methods and sources of data, it should respond to the following questions:

5.6 What kinds of data can best answer the evaluative inquiry questions we seek to answer?

5.7 What type of data will indicate if the activities, procedures, or policies in question are being implemented as intended or will inform us of any unanticipated outcomes?

5.8 What type of data will indicate if the intended outcomes of these activities, procedures, or policies in question are being realized?

For fuller consideration of the three previous questions, consider:

5.9 What data already exist that might address the evaluative inquiry questions? Where does this information reside?

5.10 What other kinds of data (e.g., background information) might be available that would address the evaluative inquiry questions?

5.11 Will data be needed on an ongoing basis, or is the need more episodic— that is, particular to a one-time situation?

5.12 What logistical constraints (methodological, time, resources) must be considered?

5.13 What resources (technical/computer expertise, expenses, equipment, personnel time, access to particular personnel, etc.) will be needed to implement each data collection activity?

Answers to these questions will help in developing a list of possible data collection methods and sources of data. For instance, customers might be surveyed or interviewed about their satisfaction with products or services (see Bourque & Fielder [1995], Edwards, Thomas, Rosenfeld, & Booth-Kewley [1996], Fink [1995], Fowler [1993], Frey & Oishi [1995], Kvale [1996], and Rubin and Rubin [1995] for more on survey and interview methods). Focus groups might be conducted with parents to learn their perspective on benefits they are receiving from a family literacy program (see Greenbaum [1997] and Morgan and Krueger [1997] for details on conducting focus groups). Additional information and perspectives might be sought by looking through the current literature or by consulting subject matter experts on a topic (e.g., see the Literature-Based Discussions strategy).

Reports might be generated from internal databases about the numbers of clients seen, overtime hours logged, or any of a multitude of variables on which organizations typically maintain data concerning their activities and operations. Wherever possible, the team is likely to want to make use of existing data sources rather than initiate the collection of new data. Often, however, additional data must be collected to address the evaluative questions. In fact, a team may decide that if it cannot devote the time and effort required to implement a particular data collection activity, it may delay the inquiry effort until more time or resources become available. One caution about using existing, readily available data is in order. If these data are marginally relevant or have questionable validity, a team should be careful in how it applies these data to making decisions about future action. *Applying learning* from data that are invalid for a particular purpose is worse than collecting no data at all. The results could be quite costly.

METHODS AND PROCEDURES FOR DATA ANALYSIS AND INTERPRETATION

Once tentative data collection methods have been established, the inquiry team will want to consider how the data will be analyzed and interpreted. It is not until we assign an interpretation and meaning to the data that they begin to inform us about what actions might be taken based on findings of the inquiry. Information, then, is data that has been assigned meaning; data become information through the process of analysis and interpretation.

Different kinds of data require varying amounts of time and expertise to analyze. In choosing a data collection method, it is important to consider what will be required to analyze the data appropriately and adequately (see Coffey and Atkinson [1996], Fitz-Gibbon and Morris [1987], Miles and Huberman [1994], Sapsford and Jupp [1996], Sirkin [1994], Wolcott [1994], and Wright [1996] for more on quantitative and qualitative data analysis). For example, tape-recorded individual interviews might be considered because they can provide the most complete account of organizational members' perspectives and experiences regarding an issue. When the evaluative inquiry team considers what will be necessary to adequately analyze these data, however, it may realize that members do not have the necessary expertise in qualitative data

STRATEGY

Literature-Based Discussions

One method of data collection that helps team members explore an issue of concern more fully is literature-based discussions. These discussions provide a means for organization members to read the same material and to discuss what they have learned in the context of the issue being studied. Literature-based discussions can challenge individuals' thinking processes, depersonalize controversial topics, and increase a team's ability to learn. Reading a book or article together also facilitates dialogue, individuals' accountability for learning, and a "thinking" mind-set that might encourage experimentation.

The process of choosing a book or article depends on the questions group members have about what needs to be learned. For example, if someone knows of a book or article that is relevant, then that material might be chosen. If team members do not know of a particular piece on the subject, they might call a local bookstore for advice, search the Web, go to a city or university library, or contact colleagues in their own or other organizations for titles.

When the team discusses the material chosen, it is most helpful if they start with a general discussion and then focus on how the material has helped them think about the particular evaluative inquiry issue. Team members might pose the following questions for one another:

◆ What do we know now, that we didn't know before?
◆ What insights do we have about the evaluative inquiry issue as a result of reading this material?
◆ What did reading this material confirm? What questions did it raise?
◆ What ideas or strategies do we want to try to use?
◆ What do we agree with/disagree with?
◆ What ideas would work in this organization and which ones wouldn't? Why do we think this?
◆ Would we recommend this material to others interested in the topic?

STRATEGY

Literature-Based Discussions (continued)

It is important to make sure that the material is read and discussed in a timely manner. Taking 3 months to read a book is probably not a good idea if reading it is to be used as a data collection method for evaluative inquiry. Team members must agree to read the material in the time period agreed upon so that their learning can be applied to the *carrying out the inquiry* phase of the project.

In summary, literature-based discussions can be quite useful as a data collection method when the issues are complex, the topic is new, opinions on the topic vary widely, and several team members lack background in the area being studied.

---

analysis or the time it requires (see Marshall and Rossman [1994] and Morse [1997] for more on the resource requirements of qualitative inquiry). The resources for data analysis that are available to the inquiry team can heavily influence choices about data collection methods. An external evaluation consultant can be particularly helpful in sorting out the relative merits and trade-offs among different data collection methods and the analyses they will require. In general, questions for the inquiry team to consider are:

5.14 How will each type of data collected be analyzed?

5.15 What expertise/resources will be needed? How much time will it take to analyze the data from each method used?

5.16 In what ways can different individuals and groups contribute to the analysis and interpretation of data?

The latter question speaks to an important consideration in how data analysis and interpretation are carried out. Typically, data analysis activities are conducted by those with evaluation or research expertise (from outside or within the organization). Interpretation of the data is also sometimes best thought to be conducted by those who have analyzed it; however, the impact and usefulness of the inquiry effort can be significantly enhanced by involving those most closely linked with designing and implementing any changes that might result from the inquiry's findings.

Data are more effectively analyzed and interpreted as a collaborative effort involving the organizational members most qualified to do so—that is, those most closely associated with the issue being explored. Although statistical analyses and summary reports might best be produced by those with technical expertise in this area, the interpretation of statistical findings should be made in working sessions with the evaluative inquiry team and members of the wider organization. These sessions use findings as a catalyst for further dialogue and reflection that go far beyond the original data, and these sessions should be considered an integral part of the ongoing inquiry. Planning for such working sessions should begin at this time. The notion of involving stakeholder groups in the interpretation (and possibly the analysis) of data may be an unfamiliar one within some organizations. Informing stakeholder groups of this upcoming opportunity to collaborate and react to inquiry findings may lessen any perceived threat relative to the inquiry effort and may enhance the use of the inquiry's findings.

METHODS AND PROCEDURES
FOR COMMUNICATING AND REPORTING

Although addressed last here, one of the most important tasks of the *carrying out the inquiry* phase is to develop a plan for communicating during the inquiry and reporting its findings. Collaboration and ongoing communication with stakeholders both within and outside the organization is key to the success of any inquiry effort. Particular individuals or groups may have any or all of the following communicating and reporting needs: (a) specific details informing them about upcoming inquiry activities, (b) progress or status reports on how inquiry activities are proceeding, (c) interim reports of findings, and (d) final reports of findings (Torres et al., 1996). Tailoring communication and reporting activities for various stakeholders may result in the following:

- Organization members may develop an increased ownership and interest in the evaluative inquiry process and findings.
- Progress or accountability of organizational operations and/or outcomes can be demonstrated.
- The inquiry findings can be used to develop policy and/or operational decisions.
- Organizational activities, functions, operations, and outcomes can be further developed, promoted, and understood.
- Support for organizational activities, functions, operations, and outcomes can be gained.

Depending on the situation, communicating and reporting can occur through a variety of formats (see Exhibit 5.1).

EXHIBIT 5.1.

Formats for Communicating and Reporting

- ▲ *Working sessions with clients and stakeholders*
- ▲ *Short written communications*
- ▲ *Personal discussions*
- ▲ *Interim/progress reports*
- ▲ *Final reports*
- ▲ *Executive summaries*
- ▲ *Chart essays*
- ▲ *Verbal presentations*
- ▲ *Newsletters, bulletins, and brochures*
- ▲ *Videotape presentations*
- ▲ *Poster sessions*
- ▲ *Public meetings*
- ▲ *News media communications*

Communicating and reporting formats that are particularly useful for *carrying out the inquiry* are working sessions, short written communications, personal discussions, and internal newsletters. For example, working sessions that incorporate opportunities for reflection and dialogue can be used to address any of the questions presented in this chapter to design and implement the data collection efforts. Short written communications such as memos, faxes, e-mail messages, or postcards are excellent ways of keeping team and other organizational members abreast of inquiry activities. Ongoing, substantive personal discussions about inquiry activities, either planned or impromptu, between individuals are one of the most powerful forms of communication and constitute part of the requisite infrastructure for any learning organization, as described in Chapter 7.

Consider the following questions when identifying the communicating and reporting needs of various stakeholders, as well as appropriate formats for communicating and reporting.

5.17 What are some different analytic or reporting frameworks that might be appropriate for representing findings from the evaluative inquiry (e.g., the original evaluative questions, some organizational or programmatic framework, a new issues-oriented framework determined by the content of the findings)?

5.18 What does each stakeholder group need to know about how the inquiry is progressing and when? What is the best format and channel for communicating this information?

5.19 In addition to the previously identified stakeholders, who else should receive communications about the inquiry?

5.20 Is a comprehensive final report necessary? Will more informal reporting suffice?

PLANNING FORMATS

To effectively manage all the tasks associated with data collection, analysis, and interpretation, and communicating and reporting, team members should develop management plans that describe the work to be done during this phase. Figure 5.1 is one example of a data collection management plan (see Payne [1994], Stake [1995], Stecher and Davis [1987], and Worthen et al. [1997] for additional approaches to formulating evaluation plans). For each inquiry method listed, space is provided for detailing (a) the steps necessary to implement the method and (b) the person(s) or team responsible, the dates/timeline, and the resources needed for each step. By referencing the evaluative questions in the column labeled "Inquiry Question #," it is ensured that each question will be addressed by at least one method of data collection. An example set of basic steps necessary to implement an employee survey is as follows.

1. Design survey.

2. Pilot and revise survey.

3. Administer survey.

4. Enter survey data into database.

5. Conduct analyses of survey data.

6. Interpret findings.

7. Develop recommendations.

A more specific set of steps might include "select sample of respondents," "draft and revise cover letter," "draft and revise follow-up procedures," "implement follow-up procedures," and so on. The evaluative inquiry team can delineate the set of data collection and analysis tasks to the level of detail deemed appropriate. For each task listed on the plan, the responsible party and dates for completion are also entered. Any of a wide variety of resources needed for each task (e.g., direct expenses, technical assistance consultation, photocopies, phone charges, clerical support) also can be listed.

Figure 5.2 provides a sample plan format for communicating and reporting the inquiry's progress and findings (see Morris, Fitzgibbon, and

DATA COLLECTION PLAN
Project Name:

Data Collection Methods	Inquiry Question #	Steps to Implement the Data Collection Method	Person(s)/Team Responsible for Step	Dates/ Timeline	Resources Needed
		1.	1.	1.	1.
		2.	2.	2.	2.
		3.	3.	3.	3.
		4.	4.	4.	4.
		5.	5.	5.	5.
		1.	1.	1.	1.
		2.	2.	2.	2.
		3.	3.	3.	3.
		4.	4.	4.	4.
		5.	5.	5.	5.
		1.	1.	1.	1.
		2.	2.	2.	2.
		3.	3.	3.	3.
		4.	4.	4.	4.
		5.	5.	5.	5.

Figure 5.1. Sample Format for a Data Collection Plan

COMMUNICATING AND REPORTING PLAN

Project Name: _____

Audiences	Communicating and Reporting Need	Format(s)	When Needed
	___ Specifics about Upcoming Inquiry Activities		
	___ Progress Report on Inquiry Activities		
	___ Interim Report of Findings		
	___ Final Report of Findings		
	___ Specifics About Upcoming Inquiry Activities		
	___ Progress Report on Inquiry Activities		
	___ Interim Report of Findings		
	___ Final Report of Findings		
	___ Specifics about Upcoming Inquiry Activities		
	___ Progress Report on Inquiry Activities		
	___ Interim Report of Findings		
	___ Final Report of Findings		

Figure 5.2. Sample Format for a Communicating and Reporting Plan

SOURCE: Adapted from *Evaluation Strategies for Communicating and Reporting: Enhancing Learning in Organizations,* Torres, Preskill, and Piontek, © 1996 by Sage Publications.

115

Freeman [1987], Posavac and Carey [1997], and Worthen et al. [1997] for additional resources on communicating and reporting). The communicating and reporting plan helps ensure that all audiences receive timely information about the inquiry relative to their needs. The first column provides space to list each different audience who may have any or all of the four communicating and reporting needs shown in the second column. The third column provides space for listing different formats (see Exhibit 5.1) for each communicating and reporting need checked. Finally, dates for delivering each format can be listed in the fourth column.

As with any plan, it is useful to develop a draft and then obtain input from a wider group of stakeholders within the organization. The process of developing the plan itself is an essential tool for involving a wide variety of organizational members and crystallizing the role of the evaluative inquiry for learning in organizations. We turn our attention now to implementing the plan for data collection, analysis, and interpretation, and communicating and reporting.

IMPLEMENTING INQUIRY ACTIVITIES

C*arrying out the inquiry* typically requires attention to myriad tasks and details. Using the data collection plan, and communicating and reporting plans just described, helps those responsible carry out the different tasks successfully. At the same time, the inquiry team monitors implementation of the inquiry to ensure that all is going smoothly. No amount of work in developing plans, however, can anticipate some events within an organization.

Data Collection

As the various data collection methods are being implemented, the team may periodically come together to ask the following questions:

5.21 Is the data collection plan being implemented as specified? If not, why not?

5.22 What new developments threaten successful implementation of the data collection activities?

5.23 How is the organization reacting to carrying out the inquiry?

5.24 What adjustments to the data collection plan need to be made?

5.25 What assumptions, values, beliefs, assumptions, and knowledge are proposed adjustments to the plan based upon?

5.26 What individuals or groups need to be apprised of adjustments made to the data collection plan?

Answers to these questions ensure that the team is doing everything possible to support the implementation of the data collection plan, and that useful data are being gathered.

Data Analysis and Interpretation

Once the data have been collected, the inquiry team analyzes and interprets the data (see the strategy Working Session to Interpret Survey Results). Based on implementing the earlier steps of the inquiry's data collection methods, analysis and interpretation activities will most likely proceed according to the original or a revised schedule. It is good to consider again, however, how this part of the inquiry is progressing.

5.27 Are analysis and interpretation activities on schedule?

5.28 Do any new developments from either within or outside the organization threaten successful implementation of analysis and interpretation activities?

5.29 What adjustments to the analysis strategies are necessary? What individuals or groups need to be apprised of these adjustments?

As analysis and interpretation proceeds, the inquiry team should also consider possible analytic frameworks or organizers that would be most

Strategy

Working Session to Interpret Survey Results

Organizations often opt to conduct written surveys that include Likert-scale items as a means of assessing attitudes and/or behaviors relative to a particular organizational function or issue. Typically, statistical averages are calculated for each of these quantitative survey items. One strategy to involve stakeholders in interpreting the results of the survey is to conduct a working session where they are asked to estimate the mean response of each survey item and explain why they have chosen that particular estimate. This activity engages their thinking about the item and provides a vehicle for uncovering their various perspectives about the survey topic. Once each member of a given stakeholder group has provided responses and the reasoning behind them, the actual results for each item are revealed. Doing so provides the focus for a second round of dialogue about the discrepancies between the estimates and the actual results. Follow these general guidelines for conducting this type of working session.

1. Conduct the working session with no fewer than 4, but no more than 10, stakeholders. Carefully consider the makeup of the group for each session. More focused and detailed dialogue is likely to occur among a group from within the same department, work area, or functional area. A more heterogeneous group can be formed to integrate and inform perspectives from across the organization.

2. Begin the working session with (a) an overview of its purpose, expected outcomes, and anticipated next steps; (b) sufficient background information to orient those present (i.e., the survey's purpose, time frame, respondent group, response rate, etc.); and (c) the opportunity for those present to ask any questions they may have.

3. Use worksheets that members of the stakeholder group complete individually at the beginning of the session to help focus the group's dialogue. The worksheet should list each survey item with space (a) to provide an estimate of the mean response for each item and (b) to write a brief explanation of the reasoning behind that estimate. Consider grouping similar items together and completing Steps 3 through 6 in turn for each group of similar items. Provide time, usually 2 to 3 minutes per item, for those present to complete the worksheet individually. Writing down

Strategy

Working Session to Interpret Survey Results (continued)

perceptions before sharing publicly lessens the possibility that members will screen their thoughts at the same time that they develop them. Have a facilitator record each person's estimates to each item on a flip chart (visible to the whole group), along with a few words that summarize the participants' reasoning.

4. After all estimates and explanations have been recorded, invite dialogue about the team's perspectives. Ask members to consider the following questions: (a) How similar/dissimilar are the estimates? (b) How similar/dissimilar are the reasons behind the estimates? (c) What accounts for the extent to which estimates and reasons vary? Depending on the number of items covered, this dialogue might last anywhere from 10 to 30 minutes.

5. Now, using a different colored marker, in a reserved space beside each item, record its actual mean.

6. Engage the group in a second round of reflection and dialogue about the discrepancies between estimates and actual results for each item, using the same kinds of questions as in Step 4 above.

7. Then, engage the group in a third round of reflection and dialogue about (a) what they have learned from the dialogues and (b) what additional questions and/or issues have been identified. Record the results of this dialogue on flip chart paper.

useful for conveying the results of the inquiry findings. That is, once analyzed, data might be organized and presented according to:

- The original evaluative inquiry questions.
- The program's goals and objectives.
- A particular logic model of a program's functioning.
- Additional issues that have emerged through the analysis and interpretation of data.
- Organizational or departmental functions.

- Parameters of a particular program or function.
- The questions on the data collection instruments (surveys, interviews).
- Recommendations, lessons learned, or indicated actions based on inquiry findings (see Framing Inquiry Findings as Lessons Learned strategy).

In considering each of these possible frameworks, the inquiry team should ask:

5.30 How well does each possible different framework meet the learning needs of the organization?

5.31 What values, beliefs, and assumptions are reflected in the choice of a particular analytic or reporting framework?

5.32 What other perspectives should be considered?

5.33 How should quantitative and qualitative data be presented?

5.34 How should data across departments or sites be integrated and presented?

As these questions are being considered by the inquiry team, some members of the team possibly will want to acquire additional input by meeting with key decision makers within the organization to (a) review how the results are expected to be used and (b) discuss the relative merits of alternative frameworks.

Developing Recommendations

Interpretation of data and the development of recommendations are closely intertwined. At the same time that the inquiry team interprets data, almost invariably its members will begin thinking about possible actions to take based on what they believe the data mean. At this point, it is important that recommendations remain somewhat general (see the illustrative case at the end of this chapter for example recommendations). That is, in many cases the results of an inquiry will not provide enough specific information to indicate precisely how a particular recommendation should be carried out. As will be explained in Chapter 6, consideration of different action alternatives for implementing the recommendations is undertaken during the *applying learning* phase of evaluative inquiry. The inquiry team's major concern now will be to make sure the recommendations it develops are truly informed by the findings and interpretations of the inquiry. Questions it should consider include

    5.35 What evidence supports each recommendation?

    5.36 Does the set of recommendations represent all findings of the inquiry?

    5.37 Do recommendations take into account what is known about organizational context, logistics, and constraints?

    5.38 What particular values, beliefs, or assumptions are reflected in each recommendation?

Communicating and Reporting

Throughout the evaluative inquiry effort, implementation of the communicating and reporting plan should be monitored and revised according to changes in other elements of the data collection plan. The communicating and reporting plan should be amended as additional audiences are identified, the effectiveness of particular formats is assessed, and the need for more detailed explanation surfaces. In particular, the inquiry team will want to consider these questions about the content and format of various communications and reports as they are developed (see Torres et al., 1996).

    5.39 Are communications and reports written in a clear, jargon-free style?

    5.40 Have tables and figures been used effectively to make information more understandable?

    5.41 Has the communication of negative findings been handled productively (e.g., within the context of continuous improvement and learning)? (See Framing Inquiry Findings as Lessons Learned strategy.)

    5.42 Have findings and interpretations been appropriately summarized for different audiences?

    5.43 Does the format of each communication/report facilitate easy interpretation and assimilation of its content?

Strategy

Framing Inquiry Findings as Lessons Learned

Organizational Research Services (ORS) was hired to conduct both a process and an outcome evaluation of the Pierce County (WA) Violence Prevention Program. The program consists of seven projects funded by the Tacoma-Pierce County Commission on Children, Youth, and Their Families. The process evaluation described how projects work and offers observations about the projects' successes and challenges. The outcome evaluation measured changes in participants' lives, or in institutions or communities. ORS's report to the commission summarized the lessons learned from both the process and outcome evaluations. Based on a 3-year review of outcome evaluation results, ORS reported the following lessons learned about the Pierce County Violence Prevention Program.

- The majority (81%) of the projects have demonstrated moderate to high levels of progress reaching some of their violence prevention outcomes.
- Projects have made improvements between Year 1 and Year 3.
- Individual outcomes had high levels of progress, family outcomes had high to moderate levels of progress, school outcomes had mostly moderate levels of progress, and community interventions had moderate to low levels of progress.

Perhaps more important, ORS reported the following additional lessons learned from both the outcome and process evaluation data. These lessons focused on critical elements of program management and development, questioning and reflection, inter- and intra-agency collaboration, and continuous improvement.

1. Good management practices must be followed.
   - ◆ Stay focused on critical activities. The right balance of resources and activities is essential to achieve good outcomes.
   - ◆ A team approach is necessary with both staff and other partners. Time for reflection and sharing needs to be part of "regular work" of programs—not a luxury.

Strategy

Framing Inquiry Findings as Lessons Learned (continued)

◆ Staff must be valued, compensated adequately, and supported.
◆ Time and effort must be devoted to staff supervision.
◆ Adequate staff training is needed.
◆ Original program designs should be maintained even when turnover in management occurs.
◆ Program improvement should be the focus, not fund development.
◆ Data collection and analysis should be an integral part of day-to-day operations and be designed as simple and practical as possible.

2. Adequate attention to program development is essential.
   ◆ Taking time to establish trust and working on "baby steps" is essential.
   ◆ The right mix of fun and growth/development is needed.
   ◆ Celebrate successes of staff and participants. Reinforce the positive steps of growth along the way.
   ◆ Need to be creative and flexible.
   ◆ Duration and intensity must be adequate and flexible.
   ◆ Program design needs to be consistently implemented.
   ◆ Program theory must match the logic model and community needs.
   ◆ Continual improvement is necessary. Projects should keep asking questions about what does and does not work, why, and what can be done about it.
   ◆ Linkages with other community organizations and residents must be established to reduce isolation, make better use of scarce resources, allow programs to build on one another, and ensure ongoing growth and development of participants. Linkages require time and effort to develop.

3. Grant management practices should be revised.
   ◆ The lessons learned should be incorporated into Request for Proposals (RFPs) and contracting. Agencies should respond only to RFPs that match their outcomes.
   ◆ Funders should look at the outcomes they are buying rather than the outputs or quantity of services bought.
   ◆ Contracts should be revised as often as needed.
   ◆ Project activities and outcomes should be discussed regularly to encourage continuous improvements.

(continued on next page)

Strategy

Framing Inquiry Findings as Lessons Learned (continued)

◆ Agencies should be encouraged to share outcomes, indicators, and results.

◆ Outcomes should be combined with other information to help determine how community resources should be allocated. Diversity and system changes should be supported.

◆ Agencies should share their lessons learned to offer guidance to others.

ORS concludes: "By following these lessons learned, continuing to evaluate process and outcomes, and striving for continued improvement, agencies and funders can tackle community goals together. Then funders will be in the position to measure progress on the community goals and determine whether current strategies are in fact making a difference."

ORS's full report summarized, in three main sections, the evidence from each of the seven projects that supported each of the 24 lessons learned above. This evidence was presented in boxed text with the lesson in bold underneath. In this way, the report brought to the surface critical issues about program operations but positioned them within an organizational learning context. This approach to communicating and reporting provided a sound basis for continued collaborative work within and between the agencies involved to apply their learning.

SOURCE: Adapted from materials developed by Organizational Research Services (1997, October). *Lessons learned from the Evaluation of the Pierce County Violence Prevention Program.* September 1994 to July 1997. Report submitted to Tacoma-Pierce County's commision on Children, Youth and Families. Seattle, WA. Used with permission.

By the end of the *carrying out the inquiry* phase, a team will have designed and implemented data collection methods, analyzed and interpreted results, and communicated and reported information about the inquiry's progress and its findings to appropriate parties within and outside the organization (see Exhibit 5.2). From the learning based on these activities, it will also likely develop a set of recommendations for further action within the organization. To illustrate what this phase of the evaluative inquiry looks like in

Exhibit 5.2. Benefits of Carrying Out the Inquiry

▲ *Provides trustworthy, credible information upon which to base actions within the organization*

▲ *Gives fuller consideration to the mutual impact of contextual/political issues and data collection activities, resulting in a more sensitive, relevant, and productive inquiry design*

▲ *Answers specific questions and reduces uncertainties about particular programs, policies, and procedures within the organization*

▲ *Provides a means for interpreting findings in terms of crucial, mediating aspects of the organization's internal and external context*

▲ *Provides a vehicle for deeper understanding of issues within the organization and further nourishes individual, team, and organizational learning*

▲ *Provides specific information (recommendations) on which to take action*

---

practice, take a look at the case example started in Chapter 4 and continued below. Chapter 6 describes the next phase of the evaluative inquiry, *applying learning.*

ILLUSTRATIVE CASE—CARRYING OUT THE INQUIRY

The next phase in the evaluative inquiry process is to have the team come together to plan how it would *carry out the inquiry*—the design of the inquiry, the kinds of data needed, the data collection and analysis methods, and the means for communicating and reporting. First, however, the team reviewed the work done in the *focusing* phase (see inquiry's purpose, stakeholders, and evaluative questions presented at the end of the case in Chapter 4).

To begin this next phase, the facilitator asked the team questions about what kind of data it would find particularly useful. Were there preferences for certain kinds of data? For example, was it important to know the stories of women who participated in the program (qualitative data)? Did the team need to know how often the service was being used and by whom (quantitative data)? She also asked if the team thought the women involved in delivering the program and those receiving the program would object to any particular data collection method. For example, would these women be inclined to respond to a survey? Would they be willing to share their stories in a focus group interview? Would they feel comfortable being interviewed on the telephone? Because the facilitator was an external consultant, not deeply familiar with the program or its clients, it was important to ask those closest to the program for their insights into how the data might best be collected.

After some discussion about possible data collection methods, the facilitator suggested that the team look back at the evaluative questions. She asked:

▲ What kinds of data can best answer the evaluative inquiry questions we seek to answer? Which questions imply the collection of words (qualitative data), and which imply the need for numbers (quantitative data)?

▲ What type of data will indicate if the activities in question are being implemented as intended, or will inform us of any unanticipated outcomes?

▲ What data already exist that might address the evaluative inquiry questions? Where does this information reside? How easily can it be accessed?

▲ What other kinds of data (e.g., background information) might be available that would address the evaluative inquiry questions?

From this dialogue, the facilitator and team members agreed that selected samples of individuals would be invited to participate in (a) focus group interviews, (b) individual interviews conducted in person and via telephone, and (c) a mailed survey. The team also decided on the number of persons needed to include in each of these samples, such that there would be sufficient data upon which to base recommendations.

Throughout this process, the facilitator asked team members what skills and experiences they had (a) in interviewing and in designing and administering surveys, and (b) with quantitative and qualitative data analysis. When it became clear that the team would need help in designing the data collection instruments and conducting interviews, she offered to assist in these tasks. It was understood, however, that team members would learn from the facilitator so they could begin to do these tasks themselves with more limited assistance in the future.

The facilitator then asked team members to consider what barriers to *carrying out the inquiry* they might encounter. They mentioned their lack of time to collect data, the lack of participants' time to provide data, some internal politics that were related to a fear of change, and a general concern about the confidentiality of data. The team identified various strategies it could use to maximize available time and minimize people's fear of change and inquiry.

Finally, the evaluative inquiry team members thought about how they could best communicate with each other and other organization members regarding progress of the inquiry effort as well as its findings. The facilitator asked questions about who should receive progress reports and who would benefit from shorter or longer final reports. Through dialogue and reflection, team members voiced their beliefs about who might be most interested in certain forms of communication and why.

From there, the team developed a data collection and communicating and reporting plan that outlined the data collection methods, anticipating analysis procedures and ways in which the team would communicate and report its progress and findings. These plans identified each of the *carrying out the inquiry* tasks, who was responsible for the task, when it was to be conducted, and any costs associated with the task. The plans clearly detailed what was to be done, by whom, and when.

At this point, team members and the facilitator were ready to go forward. Over the next 6 weeks, instruments were developed, and data were collected and analyzed. Team members kept in contact with one another through e-mail and short memos. When all the data had been analyzed, charts and tables were developed to describe the findings. Particularly helpful and insightful quotations had been highlighted in the interview transcripts and were provided to each team member. The next step was to make sense of the findings and to answer the question, "What do these findings mean?"

To guide this process, the team members who analyzed the data had each of the tables and charts enlarged and copied onto laminated poster boards. One by one, each chart was presented, and the team considered the data. A packet containing all the charts and tables was also given to each team member so they could make notes as ideas occurred to them. As the team looked at each chart, members were asked the following questions.

▲ What do these findings mean? How would you interpret them?

▲ Are any of these findings surprising to you?

▲ What are some other interpretations of these findings?

▲ What do these findings confirm?

▲ What did you expect to see in these findings, but don't?

The facilitator's job was to make sure that all the data were considered and that none of the findings were ignored. This is particularly important when certain findings are negative or disappointing. Team members spent about 4 hours interpreting the data and discussing what they were learning.

From their dialogue, they developed the following set of recommendations they believed would address the original issue of why referrals to the program were declining.

1. Continue to provide exercise information and equipment to clients.

2. Continue and expand efforts to increase the community's awareness of the program.

3. Clarify and strengthen the process by which referrals to the program are made, particularly by health care providers.

4. Consider the development of a program newsletter to be sent to volunteers, women served, and health care providers.

5. Examine the frequency and quality of volunteer training.

Not surprisingly, they learned that the decline in referrals was not due to just one cause; the issue was far more complex, thus requiring multiple actions. In Chapter 6, Applying Learning, we will see how they used what they learned from the evaluative inquiry effort to (a) generate various action alternatives for each recommendation, (b) select the best alternatives, and (c) develop action plans to implement them.

6

Applying Learning

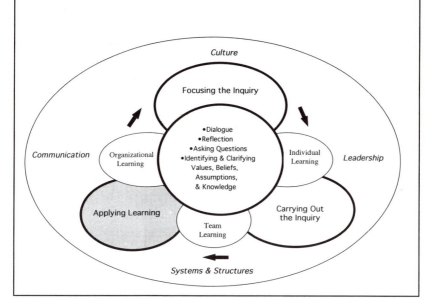

pplying learning takes place when the organization believes it has enough information to inform changes that will address the original object of the evaluative inquiry. This usually occurs when the findings and recommendations of an evaluative inquiry are available. Unfortunately, however, this phase of the inquiry process is often the most neglected—yet it is fundamental to reinforcing the cycle of continuous learning. The *applying learning* phase consists of three distinct activities:

- Identifying and selecting among action alternatives
- Developing an action plan
- Implementing the action plan and monitoring its progress

Most organizations will see the core of this phase as the action plan and its implementation (see Figure 6.1). The action plan itself might entail making minor adjustments to a program, process, or product; substantially changing an entire program's or department's purpose and procedures; or developing and implementing a completely new program. The more expansive steps undertaken before and after initial implementation of an action plan must be given adequate time and consideration. That is, a key element of successful action planning is the consideration of a variety of specific alternatives for implementing recommendations based on the findings of the *carrying out the inquiry* phase. It is indeed tempting to begin planning and committing to the specifics of a change before different possible solutions, and related issues and concerns, have been given sufficient chance to surface and become part of the planning process.

Careful deliberation of alternatives and potential solutions using the four learning processes described in this book is a critical aspect of the broader, first step—identifying action alternatives. At any one time, most individuals in an organization will have considered potential solutions to the dilemmas facing the organization—just as a matter of their own daily observations and reflections. Indeed, this kind of ongoing observation and reflection is precisely the focus of evaluative inquiry. At this point, however, organizational members are learning from the findings of a specific, systematic inquiry. These findings, along with other political, logistical, and cost considerations, will be used to identify various action alternatives, select among them, and develop an action plan to implement the alternative(s) chosen.

Once the action plan is implemented, the organization continues the inquiry process through dialogue and reflection by asking questions and identifying values, beliefs, assumptions, and knowledge—in an effort to monitor progress and make adjustments as needed. Initially, these activities will be closely tied to implementation of the action plan as written. As new issues and concerns emerge and are incorporated into

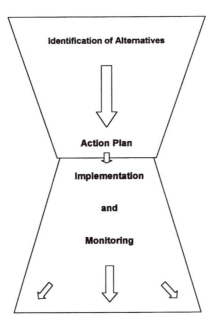

Figure 6.1. Applying Learning From the Inquiry

a continuous learning process, the scope of this effort again broadens, as illustrated in Figure 6.1. The remainder of this chapter discusses each of the three elements of *applying learning*: identifying and selecting among action alternatives, developing an action plan, and implementing the action plan and monitoring progress.

IDENTIFYING AND SELECTING ACTION ALTERNATIVES

As a result of an inquiry that has just been carried out, the team will have a set of recommendations to consider with respect to the original evaluative inquiry questions. These recommendations will vary in detail but most often will not contain much information indicating *how* the recommendation should be carried out. Depending on the scope of the inquiry, the number of recommendations can be as few as 1 and as many as 15 or 20. Most evaluative inquiries will yield between 4 and 12 recommendations, each one of which might be carried out in a variety of ways. Thus, the three activities necessary to *apply learning* discussed in this chapter are applicable to each different recommendation.

Sometimes the inquiry will have yielded more findings and recommendations than the organization can reasonably act on at once. A process of prioritizing among the recommendations likely will be appropriate. The evaluative inquiry team or a newly configured implementation team will want to begin work with the set of recommendations using these questions.

6.1 What priority should each recommendation be given (low, medium, high)?

6.2 What reasoning is behind each prioritization?

6.3 What values, beliefs, assumptions, and knowledge are reflected in reasons given?

After a period of reflection and dialogue on these questions, the team can use a method of individual voting to prioritize the recommendations. Based on their dialogue, it is likely that any original prioritization individuals might have given the set of recommendations would be somewhat or substantially changed. Averaging the ranks given by individuals in the group can produce a final prioritization. The team is then prepared to proceed with identifying action alternatives to implement the recommendation(s) that receive(s) the highest average rank(s).

In actuality, the process of identifying different action alternatives very often begins as the inquiry team and others are in the process of analyzing and interpreting data (see Chapter 5). Dialogues about what data mean almost always include mention of various ways of solving problems that the data inform. As teams worked together to analyze and interpret data, they may have recorded their early thinking about different solutions or action alternatives as a "running sidebar," visible to all participants. If available, any lists of preliminary action alternatives can be expanded on in a brainstorming session that begins with the following question:

6.4 In what possible (additional) ways can this recommendation be addressed?

At this point, two approaches can be taken. Team members can (a) engage in a broad discussion and dialogue about concerns, issues, and solutions; or (b) be asked not to concern themselves with particular implementation issues, but instead to think of and list as many different alternatives as possible. In the first approach, any response that comes to mind is appropriate. The strategy on Capturing Concerns, Issues, and Action Alternatives explains how to track and organize all the different types of information that are addressed in a freewheeling dialogue about specific recommendations.

In the second approach, creative, boundary-spanning thinking about solutions without the limitations of possible logistical and political problems is strongly encouraged. Potential implementation problems can be explored later, when each different alternative is considered in depth. The strategy on Using Technology to Facilitate Brainstorming is a good way to involve numerous organizational members in generating action alternatives. It allows for anonymity, which is likely to result in a wider variety of alternatives.

Whichever approach is taken, broad departmental or organizational involvement is particularly important at this stage, when possible actions are being considered. Organizational members who are not involved in the identification and selection of an internally initiated change have the right to feel slighted, if not resentful—particularly when the change will significantly affect their work. Such circumstances often contribute to the failure of many initiatives within organizations.

Once a broad set of alternative actions has been identified, the evaluative inquiry team will then want to consider numerous questions about each alternative.

6.5 Specifically, what will this action alternative achieve?
6.6 What groups and individuals would be involved in the implementation of this action alternative?
6.7 What other groups and individuals will be affected by it?
6.8 What are potential undesirable consequences of this alternative?

Strategy

Capturing Concerns,
Issues, and Action Alternatives

This strategy presents a means for capturing and organizing all the different concerns, issues, and ideas about possible solutions or action alternatives that might be addressed in a freewheeling dialogue about specific recommendations. A working session would be scheduled involving those persons most likely to implement any changes based on the findings and recommendations of a specific evaluative inquiry. Its purpose would be to have a dialogue about implementation of the recommendations. The session would begin with the following two-part question posed by a facilitator:

- ◆ What concerns do you have about each recommendation?
- ◆ In what possible ways might we implement each recommendation?

As the group engages in an open-ended dialogue in response to these questions, the facilitator tracks information heard in two categories: concerns/issues and action alternatives for implementing the recommendation. To do so, she uses a flip chart page divided in half and labeled with these two topics at the top of each half.

This working session might last anywhere from 90 to 120 minutes. When a lull in the dialogue occurs and it appears that the group's ideas and concerns have been fully expressed, the facilitator reviews and summarizes what she has captured on the flip chart pages. At this point, the lists of concerns/issues and action alternatives can be verified with the group and modified according to any additional input. The session ends with planning for a subsequent session where concerns/issues will be linked with possible solutions.

6.9 How much will implementation of this action cost? What other resources will it require?

6.10 What new skills, knowledge, and attitudes will organizational members need to ensure this action's success?

6.11 What incentives are there for organizational members to make the changes in their daily practices that it will require?

STRATEGY

Capturing Concerns, Issues, and Action Alternatives (continued)

In preparation for the second session, a matrix is constructed with action alternatives listed on one axis and concerns/issues listed on the other. The work of the group during the second session is to check off which concerns/issues are adequately addressed by each action alternative. First, group members work on the matrix individually, and then each person presents his or her results during a round of dialogue. (At this time, additional action alternatives and/or concerns/issues may arise and can be added to the matrix.) After dialogue in which individuals give their reasoning for each check mark they propose, the group comes to consensus on a final matrix. The result is a group-constructed matrix where some alternative actions have more check marks beside them than others. This forms the basis for prioritization and possible selection of a specific solution. Again, this working session ends with clear plans about the group's next steps—most likely to begin development of an action plan to implement the alternative(s) chosen.

6.12 To what extent will the organization's existing infrastructure (culture, leadership, modes of communication, other systems and structures; see Chapter 7) either support or undermine implementation of this action alternative?

6.13 Conversely, what impact will it likely have on any elements of the infrastructure?

6.14 In what groups, teams, departments, and/or individuals is this action alternative likely to be met with resistance?

6.15 What additional obstacles or barriers, if any, might impede successful implementation? What could be done to overcome any of these barriers?

6.16 What has been the organization's experiences with similar change initiatives?

Addressing the above questions for each action alternative might require some background work that individuals or subgroups could

Strategy

Using Technology to Facilitate Brainstorming

Using a technology called "groupware" is an efficient and effective means for obtaining individuals' opinions and ideas in an anonymous manner within a group setting. The method is particularly helpful in generating discussion about a group's responses, which are displayed on a monitor at the front of the room. The way it works is as follows:

- The facilitator poses a question to the group. (Typically, these questions have been determined ahead of time.)
- People anonymously type in their responses.
- If the responses are numerical, the software program automatically aggregates the data and displays descriptive statistics in addition to graphs and charts.
- If the responses are in the form of words, the ideas are listed, and participants then look for themes and patterns in the data.
- Participants discuss the implications and meanings of the data.

Using an electronic medium such as groupware has the following *advantages*:

- Verbatim data can be obtained simultaneously from participants.
- More ideas are generated through this medium than through traditional brainstorming techniques.
- Individuals are less fearful of their opinions being judged negatively.
- It allows people who are reticent to speak up in a group to be heard. People are more willing to state how they really think or feel about the topic.
- It can increase team members' ownership of the outcomes.
- It can serve as a catalyst for discussing "undiscussables" or highly political or sensitive topics.
- It allows people to free-associate ideas and develop a common language around key concepts.

STRATEGY

Using Technology to Facilitate Brainstorming (continued)

- Participants do not forget their ideas when waiting for their turn, as is possible in other brainstorming or focus group discussions.
- Depending on the system used, it can involve members who are not in the same geographic place or time zone.
- It can involve a larger number of participants than traditional brainstorming groups.

Some of the *disadvantages* associated with this kind of technology are:

- People who are not yet comfortable with computer technology may not be willing or able to participate.
- Verbal conversation may be limited if the facilitator does not balance the use of the technology with discussion of the ideas generated.
- Some keyboarding skills are required.
- The cost of the software can be prohibitive.
- Some may view the anonymity of responses as inappropriate in the context of community building and dialogue.
- The medium may not be suitable for all topics that need to be discussed.

undertake. They would then report back to the larger team with a summary of advantages and disadvantages for each alternative. If numerous alternatives are being considered, the larger inquiry team might then want to develop and use a means for scoring each alternative. Organizations may have particular decision-making processes they would use for arriving at a final choice of an action alternative. For instance, based on averaging scores, the original list of possibilities might be reduced to the top two or three, which are then given further consideration by the organization's highest levels of leadership.

DEVELOPING AN ACTION PLAN

Once a set of actions has been determined and the dedicated action planning process begins, identifying barriers to implementation and developing plans for minimizing them is essential. Again, of particular concern is the fact that implementation of an action plan almost invariably requires the participation of a wider range of organizational members than have been involved in the prior inquiry phases. Care must be taken to proceed with planning in such a way that other organizational members can approximate the same ownership to the plan as have its original developers. In fact, although the initial action planning work may involve a core group, it should progress with the involvement of as many organizational members as possible. For instance, action planning sessions might be held with each department involved (or representatives, in the case of very large organizations) to present a draft plan for their review, discussion, and modification. This process can be very fruitful for identifying (a) organizational members' values, assumptions, and beliefs regarding key elements of the plan; (b) barriers to implementation unknown to the original action planning group; and (c) necessary training, information, and support for the action. Obviously, the bigger the change in behavior the action requires of organizational members, the more training and support will be needed.

One way to help organization members plan for the successful implementation of an evaluative inquiry action plan is through the use of the electronic medium called "groupware" (see Strategy on Using Technology to Facilitate Brainstorming). This medium facilitates a variety of group activities—from anonymous polling and voting, to building consensus and resolving conflicts. Most systems link laptop computers together via a local area network with a monitor positioned at the front of the room. Groupware allows organization members to interact electronically with one another and the facilitator. An example of using this technology is reported by Clark and Koonce (1995), who describe a large utility company's experience in implementing a new financial management system. The company wanted to introduce this new system in a way that would help employees become committed to it. The organization's leaders decided to use technology to develop the goals and objectives of the system's implementation and to set priorities. In a focus group interview, attendees answered key questions that addressed the new system's most important functions for managing costs. Next, the group ranked 11 key items identified as critical to the system's effective implementation. Finally, the group came up with a list of behaviors and practices that needed to be changed to ensure effective implementation. The authors state:

> Groupware served as an important catalyst in helping members of a cross-functional group of top executives envision their roles as sponsors of change in their organization. It helped them create an action plan to establish processes and practices to support and sustain effective implementation of the new system. And all that was accomplished in less than one business day. (p. 36)

Any action plan should include a clear delineation of specific activities or tasks, persons/departments responsible, timelines, and means for gauging success. Most organizations already use a variety of project management planning tools that detail discrete steps for implementing a new program or process—the particulars of what, who, when, and where—so this should not be an unfamiliar task to many (see strategy on Developing an Action Plan).

As the team develops the plan, it is important that it consider all the information about the action chosen that was assembled during the previous step of identifying and selecting that action. This will help ensure that critical implementation issues are addressed in the plan—such as realistic timelines, areas where the action is likely to encounter resistance, appropriate means for introducing the action throughout a large organization, and adequate support and training. The team can use the following questions as a basis for developing an action plan.

Strategy

Developing an Action Plan

Action plans should communicate *what* action will be taken, by *whom* it will be taken, *how* it will be taken, *where* it will be taken, and *when* it will be taken. Whenever possible, it is a good idea to anticipate who should be invited to the action planning meeting. If certain individuals are likely to be asked to carry out certain actions, it is advisable for them to be present at this meeting so they have a voice in the actions identified and assigned. The process for working through the development of action plans can be more easily facilitated as a collaborative activity by using the following organizing strategy.

1. The facilitator of the meeting hangs up five pieces of flip chart paper, each titled one of the following: "What?" "Who?" "How?" Where?" and "When?"

2. The facilitator names one of the actions the team has agreed upon implementing. For example, let's say the team has decided to develop and implement a "Train the Trainer" program for its volunteer staff.

3. On the "What?" page, the team brainstorms a list of actions that need to be taken to implement this process. Some of the actions the team identifies include the following.

    a. Contact professional trainers to determine the appropriate content of a "Train the "Trainer" training program.

    b. Ask a professional trainer to critique the current volunteer training program.

    c. Design and develop the "Train the Trainer" program.

    d. Identify who will receive the "Train the Trainer" training.

    e. Determine timeline for "Train the Trainer" volunteer training.

4. The team repeats Step 3 for each of the other sheets of paper. (For example, on the "Who?" page, the team brainstorms who might be able to carry out each of the actions listed.)

5. When all five lists are complete, the responses to each question are transferred to an action plan document and distributed to each of the team members as well as to any persons listed on the "Who?" page.

6.17 What steps are necessary to carry out this action alternative? Are there several broad categories of action, each of which has smaller substeps?

6.18 How will the critical issues for successful implementation (outlined in the previous phase of identifying and selecting the action alternative) be accounted for in these steps?

6.19 Who should be responsible for carrying out each step/substep?

6.20 What amount of time realistically will be required to do so?

6.21 Are there critical organizational events that must be accounted for in developing the timeline for implementation?

Once these details of the plan have been developed through a process of dialogue and reflection, the evaluative inquiry team can address three other critical questions for each action.

6.22 How will we know if the action is being implemented successfully?

6.23 At what point(s) should dialogues to monitor progress take place?

6.24 Who should be involved in these dialogues?

The team will want to outline the answers they develop in response to these two sets of questions in a written plan. The example action planning format we offer in Figure 6.2 is very similar to the sample format for a data collection plan shown in Chapter 5 (Figure 5.1). That is, it begins in the first column with "steps to implement" and continues with columns for person(s)/team responsible, dates/timeline, and resources needed. Additional columns address critical aspects of developing the plan discussed above—identifying (a) how the team will know if implementation of each step is successful, (b) dates for progress monitoring checkpoints, and (c) who should be involved.

Although organizations may take a paper-and-pencil approach to constructing the action plan, many commercially available software products can streamline this process. They vary in complexity, with some offering sophisticated project management features. Our concern in this book, however, is not so much with the mechanical aspects of constructing the written action plan as it is with the organization's thinking and learning processes that undergird the content of the plan. (See Frame [1995], Graham and Englund [1997], Greer [1996], and Wysocki, Beck, and Crane [1995] as additional resources on action planning and project management.)

The action plan that the team agrees on at this point should be seen as both evolutionary and process-oriented. That is, once a plan is developed and implemented, team members continue to reflect on their learning along the way, and revise, update, expand, or change the plan as needed. As Young and Dixon (1996) advise, "The point is not to get the perfect plan but rather to learn to use action planning as a lifelong tool for learning and increasing effectiveness" (p. 20).

IMPLEMENTING THE ACTION PLAN
AND MONITORING PROGRESS

During implementation, a team might be tempted to feel that its work is over. After having invested substantial energy in the two previous phases of inquiry and planning specific actions, the need to rest is not surprising. An organization's enduring faith in inquiry as a means of continuous learning is critical at this point. By monitoring the initiative's implementation, organization members come to understand where, why, and with whom the action or change is or is not being implemented as planned.

Based on the dates of the progress monitoring checkpoints detailed in the action plan, the team convenes to discuss how well implementation is going. This team might be made up of members of the original inquiry team as well as representatives of the departments or units that are being affected by the action. Beginning with the "evidence of successful implementation" detailed in the action plan (see Figure 6.2), the evaluative inquiry process continues by developing additional questions about the ways in which the program is being implemented. For example, the following questions might be raised.

6.25 How is actual implementation paralleling intended implementation, and what can we learn from any discrepancies?

ACTION PLAN

Project Name

Steps to Implement	Person/Team Responsible for Implementation	Dates/Timeline	Resources Needed	Evidence of Successful Implementation	Dates for Program Monitoring	Persons/Teams Responsible for Progress Monitoring

Figure 6.2. Sample Format For an Action Plan

6.26 What new issues are surfacing that impact the success of the change being made?

6.27 What adjustments to the plan are necessary, and what is the best way to make them?

6.28 What barriers or obstacles are impeding full implementation?

Regardless of how well the plan is designed, the team will most assuredly experience challenges to its implementation. For this reason, progress monitoring is essential. All too often, organization members assume or hope that other employees will have little trouble responding to the changes required by the planned actions. Challenges to implementation arise through a wide variety of organizational and personal issues. Young and Dixon (1996, p. 25) identify four types of such "turbulence:" work/system level, work/job specific, personal, and psychological (see Exhibit 6.1).

An example of such a challenge might be a situation where an organization is attempting to implement a new performance management system that involves new procedures for providing developmental feedback as well as a basis for team- or department-wide salary increases. After a period of time, the team convenes to discuss how well implementation of the action plan is proceeding. A team member says that she believes people are not using the procedures specified in the new system. In fact, she thinks part of the problem is that many managers do not even know how to implement the new system; as a result, it is not being used as intended. Team members ask her questions that uncover the values, assumptions, beliefs, and knowledge that have led her to these conclusions. They challenge (always in a respectful way) how she has come to develop these understandings and on what evidence they are based. The process continues with other team members articulating how well they think implementation is going. Each member's observations are discussed in ways that eventually help to clarify, as much as possible, the different ways implementation is being viewed. Through this process, the team members develop new insights into their own and others' understanding of the action's implementation. Consequently, the group is much clearer regarding what steps to

EXHIBIT 6.1.

Challenges to Successful Implementation of Action Plans

Work/System Level

▲ *Reorganization*
▲ *Merger/culture change*
▲ *Downsizing*
▲ *New CEO/leadership*

Work/Job Specific

▲ *New job—same organization*
▲ *New job—new region*
▲ *New job—promotion*
▲ *Lost job—downsizing*
▲ *New job—new organization*

Personal

▲ *Family member ill*
▲ *Physical problems*
▲ *Death in family*
▲ *Separated from spouse/children*
▲ *Family counseling*

Psychological

▲ *Depression*
▲ *Alcoholism*
▲ *Chemical imbalance*
▲ *Emotional roller coaster, mood swings*

SOURCE: Adapted from *Helping Leaders Take Effective Action: A Program Evaluation,* Young and Dixon, © 1996 Center for Creative Leadership.

Strategy

Solving Implementation Issues

Given the fact that actions taken as a result of inquiry often require some kind of change, it is not surprising that a team might encounter obstacles in implementing some of the actions from its plan. As team members monitor the implementation of various actions, it is helpful for them to come together periodically to figure out ways to address implementation obstacles. The following strategy is one way for a team to brainstorm possible solutions to implementation barriers in a short period of time.

1. The facilitator asks team members to identify situations in which they believe implementation of the actions outlined in the action plan are not proceeding as planned. After a period of dialogue and reflection that confirms that the issue does exist, the facilitator writes each problem on a piece of flip chart paper.

2. For each problem, working on one at a time, team members are asked to silently write down four ideas for solving the problem.

3. As soon as everyone has listed four ideas, they exchange their sheet of paper with another person and add two more ideas. Team members then trade their papers again with a different person.

4. This process is repeated for about 15 minutes or until team members run out of ideas to address the implementation problem.

5. Each person's list is then discussed, and additional actions for resolving the issue are identified, and individual team members are designated to follow up on specific actions. These actions might involve meeting with a particular person, writing a memo, or providing additional documentation to clarify the original action. The team also might decide to revise the original action.

By being aware of implementation issues, the team can be sure that the results of its inquiry will be used as intended and will be able to learn where and why the actions taken actually do or do not have their intended affect.

SOURCE: Adapted from *Facilitator's Guide to Participatory Decision-Making*, S. Kaner, © 1996 New Society Publishers.

take if adjustments to the action plan are necessary (see strategy for Solving Implementation Issues). At the same time, they may as easily conclude that all is going well and decide to continue the current implementation strategy.

Sometimes, however, usually after a sufficient period of time, the team will decide that additional information is needed to determine if implementation has been successful and if the initiative is achieving its intended outcomes. In these situations, the team initiates the first two phases of evaluative inquiry (see Chapters 4 and 5), though likely on a much smaller scale than for the original inquiry. When this occurs, the organization cycles back though the three phases of evaluative inquiry, which further reinforces a process of continuous learning and improvement.

In the *applying learning* phase, team members have prioritized a set of recommendations based on the findings of their evaluative inquiry, identified various action alternatives for implement each recommendation, selected at least one action alternative for each recommendation, developed an action plan, and begun implementing and monitoring its progress (see Exhibit 6.2). Based on ongoing progress monitoring, individuals, teams, and the organization continue to learn about the effectiveness and impact of their practices.

ILLUSTRATIVE CASE—APPLYING LEARNING

When the team convened to apply what it learned from the inquiry, it again referred back to the purpose of the effort, which was to:

> determine the extent to which the program is meeting the needs of women it is serving and to explore ways in which the program can be improved.

They then posted the recommendations for action the team had developed from carrying out the evaluative inquiry:

1. Continue to provide exercise information and equipment to clients.

2. Continue and expand efforts to increase the community's awareness of the program.

3. Clarify and strengthen the process by which referrals to the program are made, particularly by health care providers.

4. Consider the development of a program newsletter to be sent to volunteers, women served, and health care providers.

5. Examine the frequency and quality of volunteer training.

When the team next came together, its job was to take the recommendations and develop a plan for action. To begin the process, the

EXHIBIT 6.2.

Benefits of Applying Learning

▲ *Provides for judicious, carefully reasoned selection among action alternatives*

▲ *Provides a means for understanding the implications of various potential actions*

▲ *Provides a means for developing realistic, contextually sensitive action plans*

▲ *Allows for the exploration of potential barriers or obstacles to implementing the inquiry's recommendations*

▲ *Ensures that those potentially affected by the actions are involved in planning for implementation*

▲ *Ensures that the findings from inquiry are being used to support individual, team, and organizational learning*

▲ *Reinforces an organization's focus on continuous improvement and learning throughout implementation*

facilitator, this time a team member, asked each person to think about how they would prioritize the five recommendations—which ones are most critical right now? The facilitator asked team members to reflect on why they thought particular recommendations should be addressed before others. After a few minutes, each person shared his or her thoughts about the recommendations. Important in this dialogue was understanding each person's reasoning (values, beliefs, assumptions, and knowledge) for prioritizing the recommendations the way they had. Once everyone had shared their ideas, the team considered where there was agreement and disagreement. Through another period of dialogue, they agreed on a preliminary ordering of recommendations. This prioritization did not mean that some recommendations would not be addressed; it just meant that some would get attention sooner rather than later.

The next task was to identify several action alternatives for implementing each recommendation. Looking at the first recommendation, the team began a brainstorming process that revealed a variety of ways the recommendation could be carried out (i.e., various action alternatives). After exhausting the team's ideas, members examined each action alternative, discussing possible benefits, any barriers to implementing it, who would be involved in its implementation, and the likelihood that the action alternative would have the intended effect on improving the program's visibility and referral rate. The team spent a considerable amount of time on this task, as members realized that this was what the entire inquiry process came down to—acting on what they had learned about how to improve the program. The culmination of these discussions resulted in a vote on the best action alternatives and the development of an action plan that detailed (a) the steps for implementing the action alternative chosen, (b) when each step was to be implemented and by whom, (c) the resources needed, and (d) who on the team would be responsible for monitoring its progress.

By the end of this meeting, each team member was clear about how the results of the inquiry would be used to improve the program. They each had participated in a process that tapped their knowledge and understandings, and each had contributed to strategizing the future of the program. They also knew their role in making the changes happen.

Throughout the next 6 months, the team stayed in contact with one another via e-mail and monthly meetings. During this time, they shared their observations about how the strategies were being implemented and any obstacles they thought might be impeding successful implementation. On two occasions, team members expressed concern about two program managers who seemed not to be committed to the changes. In each case, a team member volunteered to meet with the program manager to discuss the manager's perspective on various aspects of the change and to explain why it was being made. They related further details of the evaluative inquiry process they had used, why they had chosen to implement the particular strategy, and how important the individual was in ensuring that the strategy be successful. In both of these situations, team members observed improvements in the strategy's implementation after these meetings.

At the end of the 6 months, the team decided to conduct a more systematic inquiry to determine the extent to which the chosen strategies actually had made a difference in the program's viability and referral rate. The members agreed that this inquiry need not be as extensive as the first and chose to focus it on only two evaluative questions. This decision had cycled them back to the focusing the inquiry phase of the evaluative inquiry process.

CHAPTER 7

Building the Infrastructure for Evaluative Inquiry

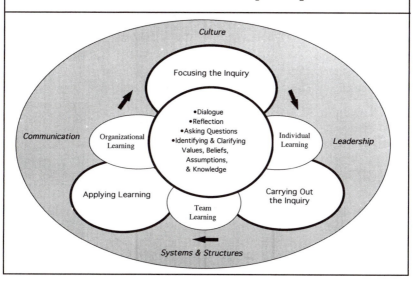

n large part, the success of evaluative inquiry is based on an organization's infrastructure, that is, the strength of the underlying foundation or framework for supporting learning within the organization. An organization's infrastructure can strongly influence the extent to which organization members learn from evaluative inquiry and use their learning to support personal and organizational goals.

One way of looking at an organization's infrastructure is to imagine it as a series of highways and byways—much like a city's road system. If we consider how people navigate through their community we see that a town's roadway system is made up of multiple-lane highways; one-way and dead-end streets; dirt as well as paved roads; roads that have signs indicating the need to stop, yield, and go; small one-lane and multiple-lane bridges; and four-way uncontrolled intersections. From an aerial view, a city's highway infrastructure looks much like a giant webbed network. This network not only allows people to get from point A to point B but also communicates the rules of driving.

We use the highway metaphor for describing the importance of organizational infrastructure because many organizations undergoing transformational change or those trying to become learning organizations have characterized their efforts as a journey (Driscoll & Preskill, 1996; Preskill, 1991; Watkins & Marsick, 1996). Although various modes of transportation are used to illustrate these change efforts, in each case, organization members have searched for a map that would guide them toward success. Like a highway system that depends on clear linkages and signage, a learning infrastructure requires the development of a systems approach to organizational design and management. Consistent with what is required for successful implementation of evaluative inquiry, systems thinking focuses on processes, views work functions as interrelated and interdependent, and reflects a commitment to working on small, well-focused actions that can produce important improvements. "An organization that is being managed as a system addresses its business issues through systemic analysis, systemic solutions, and systemic execution of those solutions" (Brache & Rummler, 1997, p. 70). In this chapter, we explore four components of an organization's infrastructure: (a) culture, (b) leadership, (c) communication, and (d) systems and structures. The nature of these components provides the foundation on which evaluative inquiry efforts can be undertaken and sustained.

CULTURE

"The culture in which . . . learning occurs—the frame-work, atmosphere, environment, set of circumstances—is the compelling determinant of the type or quality of learning" (Hoffman & Withers, 1995, p. 463). Without a culture that rewards learning, evaluative inquiry's benefits will be significantly diminished. Culture is "a set of basic tacit assumptions about how the world is and ought to be that a group of people share and that determines their perceptions, thoughts, feelings, and, to some degree, their overt behavior" (Schein, 1996, p. 11). Researchers on organizational change and educational reform have found that a precursor to real structural change in organizations is a change in culture. Culture is what undergirds all organizational life and is what influences individual learning and performance. It

> influences the way people treat and react to each other. It shapes the way people feel about the company and the work they do; the way they interpret and perceive the actions taken by others; the expectations they have regarding changes in their work or in the business; and how they view those changes. (Carleton, 1997, p. 68)

Building on our highway infrastructure metaphor, we see culture as the laws of the road. As we travel through our work day, we encounter "signs" that tell us to speed up, slow down, or yield to others, as well as traffic jams that try our patience, toll booths that require payment, roads that are closed because of repair work or natural disasters, and hills and valleys that challenge our vehicles' ability to function smoothly. If the organization's culture provides a set of laws (policies) or directions (procedures) that present barriers to learning, the journey toward becoming a learning organization, especially through evaluative inquiry, will be bumpy and brief. If the infrastructure ensures smooth, paved roads, however, evaluative inquiry processes have the potential of becoming routinized and a matter of habit. Lorrie Saito, a training specialist at Land O' Lakes, explains what having a learning culture means to her.

When I think about learning organization . . . it's not really something you have to think about or it's not exceptional, but this is just what we do in our company, and that is we create environments where people want to continue to learn something new. It doesn't have to be something big, but just day by day there's something that you can add to your repertoire or your knowledge base. My idea is that people want to try new things that are creative—which is encouraged, and there's no risk involved. I mean, there's always risk, but it's not detrimental. They can make a mistake along the way, and if this happens, we ask what can we learn? (LS, LOL: 144)

Although developing a learning culture in an organization is no small endeavor, it is a fundamental characteristic of organizations that learn from the collective experiences of their members (see Exhibit 7.1). Although it has not conducted any formal evaluation, Mike Rogowski at Ford believes that much of his division's financial turnaround in the last few years is attributable to a shift toward having a learning culture. A learning culture requires that individuals be willing to take risks, that they view mistakes as opportunities for learning, and that a climate of trust and courage supports learning through risk taking.

Taking Risks and Valuing Mistakes

Organizational learning through evaluative inquiry is all about taking risks—risks that involve raising issues, asking questions, and making changes. Risks should be considered precursors to learning; taking risks catapults us to the next level of learning. Herein lies the challenge. How do we reward risk taking when a project ends in "failure?" Perhaps it is grounded in how we define failure. For example, Sohiro Honda, founder of Honda Motors, says, "To me, success can only be achieved through

EXHIBIT 7.1.

---

*Organizational Culture That
Supports Evaluative Inquiry*

▲ *Appreciates what is best about individuals and generates hope*
▲ *Engenders trust among coworkers*
▲ *Supports risk taking and reduces fear of failure*
▲ *Rewards courage*
▲ *Values lessons learned from mistakes*

---

repeated failure and introspection," or as Thomas Watson, founder of IBM, said, "If you want to succeed, double your mistake rate" (quoted in Bryner & Marcova, 1996, pp. 76-77).

Marvin Weisbord (1987), a well-known manager and consultant who has written widely on the topic of organizational change, remembers when he first understood the significance of employee involvement in the 1960s. He was then an executive vice president of a printing technology and direct mail marketing firm that his father had founded in the early 1940s. After reading about new management theories and experiencing the hard knocks of business management, he had a revelation:

> I understood, really understood, that the essence of effective organization was *learning*, not coercing and controlling output. I realized that it took time; required real problems to be solved; involved trial, error, give, take, and experimentation. Above all, it generated tremendous anxiety. . . . With a shock I realized that the way we had been running our business was antilearning. We had no tolerance for mistakes. . . . Instead of giving people learn-

ing time, I leaped to solutions. I did not understand the subtle connections among learning, self-esteem, and productivity. (p. 13)

Relatedly, Barrett (1995) explains, "Executives are beginning to see that perhaps their most important task is the creation of learning cultures—contexts in which members explore, experiment in the margins, extend capabilities, and anticipate customers' latent needs" (p. 36). For these individuals, risk taking is a learning process in which every failure is perceived only as an opportunity to improve either in future actions or in one's immediate thinking.

As jobs are eliminated, as competition for resources increases, and as more people jockey for promotion in flat organizations, the fear of personal failure is growing. The irony is that without taking informed chances, organizations run the greater risk of going out of business or failing to provide adequate services and systems for society members. Some management writers believe that in many organizations, this fear of failure "remains the dominating motivational force of everyday life" (Bryner & Marcova, 1996, p. 76). If organization members are afraid to ask questions for fear of looking incompetent or foolish, or are seen as challenging authority or the status quo, learning from evaluative inquiry efforts will not succeed. Instead of a culture penalizing individuals for learning, the culture should support those who dare to question and who learn from their mistakes and failures. One reason people risk trying new behaviors or making their thoughts public is because they believe their efforts will be rewarded or at least appreciated and understood. In these organizations, a climate of trust and courage predominates.

Trust and Courage

Trust in each other as well as in leaders is critical for organizational learning through evaluative inquiry. Trust "consists of a willingness to increase your vulnerability to another person whose behavior you cannot control, in a situation in which your potential benefit is much less than your potential loss if the other person abuses your vulnerability" (Zand,

1997, p. 91). Unfortunately, when employees talk about trust within their organizations, often it is framed negatively with comments such as "I won't say anything because I don't trust her" or "How can you trust him when you know he'll tell so and so, and make life difficult for you?" Few would argue against the premise that changing environmental conditions in many organizations have eroded trust among employees. Life in today's organizations is less predictable, more political, and at times more risky.

When employees mistrust one another, their full capabilities go unused. Their energies are channeled into defensive routines that camouflage their knowledge and skill resources. "Mistrust weakens relationships, bringing to them suspicion and deception" (Zand, 1997, p. 89). Mistrust occurs when there is secrecy, withholding, or delaying or censoring of information, or when one's actions contradict one's words. Clearly, when mistrust occurs within an evaluative inquiry team, members are unlikely to engage openly in dialogue about their personally held values, beliefs, and assumptions. At Ford Motor Company, Krista Schulte, a team leader for Product Launches, explains how difficult it is for people to trust one another:

> I think it has taken some fearless people to come out and take the first step and share some things in front of the group and share some bad things that they've done. "You know, people, I really screwed this up. You know, I lost two hundred thousand dollars just like that. Sorry." And for that person to be rewarded with "Thank you for sharing that lesson with us." End of story. And it has to be very visible. . . . I think that's how you develop trust. (KS, Ford: 41)

The development of trusting relationships takes courage and often happens incrementally as a result of mutual practice. As one person trusts another and finds justification in her trust, she may trust again. Cindy Wakefield, a senior education consultant at the Colorado Department of Education, describes how she is navigating her way through a developing culture of trust:

I haven't gotten in trouble yet . . . but I tend to question things a lot and be very vocal about questioning them, and it doesn't really matter who is in the audience. I'll still bring something up or say something if I feel like it needs to be said. And for like the first 5 years that I worked here I kept waiting for someone to tell me my job was eliminated and be invited to go elsewhere, but that hasn't really happened. In fact I've gotten the message from the people in my unit and my supervisor and the unit director and even the commissioner and the assistant commissioner, that that kind of attitude is valued . . . that's the way that they would like CDE to move toward as opposed to it being something that would get you in trouble. (CW, CDE: 354)

As Cindy continues to be reinforced for asking questions, she may increasingly trust her colleagues, leaders, and the organization. This incremental approach to developing trusting relationships is indeed more realistic than expecting trust to be developed overnight. When people in an organization trust each other, it is likely the result of several factors that include

- the consistent application of principles
- explanations for actions taken
- the availability of status reports and forecasts
- realistic commitments made by leaders
- individuals' knowledge being shared and celebrated
- the interests of people who are not present being protected
- employees being informed about the organization's status and initiatives
- mistakes being seen as opportunities for learning—employees are not punished
- opportunities being provided for employees to give and receive feedback
- action following from feedback

LEADERSHIP

Evaluative inquiry and organizational learning will not succeed if the organization's leadership is indifferent or hostile to establishing learning processes and systems. All too often, leaders have read the latest book on a new management strategy, have brought the book into the office and told others to read it, and told them to "make it happen." In many cases, managers may then struggle to implement new approaches such as evaluative inquiry, but they frequently fail to show others what the new behaviors or practices look like. This leads to organization members' distrust of the leader's seriousness about the new strategy.

Leaders cannot change culture by tinkering with the organization's structure, by introducing new initiatives, or by laying off or firing people. Carleton (1997) worries that executives understand little about the importance of organizational culture as they implement changes. He recounts an experience in which a CEO told him he wanted to improve "corporate culture" by "putting in" a good culture. The CEO explained that his company did not yet have a culture, because his managers "had not yet gotten around to developing one" (pp. 68-69).

This anecdote helps to illustrate that leadership does in fact occur at all levels within an organization's structure. It emanates from teachers in the classroom, from first-line supervisors in a manufacturing plant, from a state department's clinical social workers, and from nurses in hospital settings. The old leadership model that focused on a single leader who set the organization's direction, made key decisions, and led the troops is now obsolete according to many management theorists. Instead of this individualistic and nonsystemic worldview, which has dominated Western management practices for decades, the new and emerging model calls for an integrated, pluralistic approach to leadership (Fullan, 1993; Senge, 1990a, 1990b, 1996; Van de Ven & Grazman, 1995).

Leadership support for evaluative inquiry must come from the very top of the organization, but also from leadership within the organization.

EXHIBIT 7.2.

Organizational Leadership
That Supports Evaluative Inquiry

▲ *Values diversity of employees and seeks pluralistic understandings*
▲ *Develops and maintains processes that support employees' ongoing learning*
▲ *Develops and supports the implementation of systems to capture employee learning and make it accessible to others in the organization*
▲ *Is more concerned with serving the organization than with seeking personal power*
▲ *Values information from inside and outside the organization*
▲ *Involves employees in the development of a learning vision*
▲ *Communicates a clear and consistent learning vision for the organization*
▲ *Translates the learning vision into achievable goals and objectives*
▲ *Models and champions ongoing learning*

In the next two sections, we address leadership as it relates to evaluative inquiry and organizational learning at these two levels.

Executive Leadership

Executive leaders develop learning infrastructures and are seen as models of new learning behaviors and norms. Leaders who strive to develop learning organizations must truly live learning. They must (a) develop and communicate a consistent learning vision and (b) model and champion learning efforts. Leaders committed to learning work hard to develop a learning vision that helps organization members know what to focus on, where to put their resources, and how to choose to accept or reject different opportunities. The vision must be one that communicates not only what the organization wants to be but also how it will get there. It must be translatable into objectives that organization members can achieve. The organization's vision must also relate to individual unit or department visions so that the organization's efforts are pointed in similar directions.

One barrier to an organization's ability to change is its inability to translate a vision into practices and accomplishments—What does it look like? How will it feel? How do we get there? An example is provided by Cindy Wakefield at the Colorado Department of Education. Here, she describes her unit's mission:

A cultural norm of Prevention Initiatives is that we are a team, and we work as a team. Our mission says that we collaborate with people within the department and people out in the field. We work with communities. We build capacity. We don't provide service; we build capacity so that people can learn to do things for themselves. Somebody who kind of wants to go off and help people by themselves wouldn't really be a useful part of the team. It might be useful in another discipline perhaps, but not in prevention and not in Prevention Initiatives. (CW, CDE: 353)

Leaders of learning organizations involve organization members in the development of a learning vision. They actively work to ensure that the organization's systems and structures support the vision's implementation throughout the organization.

Lauris Woolford, Vice-President of Mercantile Stores University in Ohio, explains how CEO David Nichols *models and champions learning*:

Mr. Nichols models learning by encouraging all managers to actively seek out learning opportunities inside and outside of Mercantile Stores. Four years ago, only a few Senior Managers attended outside classes. By attending class himself, Mr. Nichols "walks the talk" for all associates. In the beginning he agreed that if we were going to adopt a particular set of leadership practices, then it had to begin with him. Not only did he participate, (including challenging physical activities), but he led the way for less experienced managers. (LW: personal communication, October 13, 1997)

At Visteon (Ford Motor), Bob Womac, Vice-President of Operations, is known to attend 10-hour quarterly product launch team meetings, and he regularly attends the learning organization 5-day course that is offered several times a year. He introduces himself to participants as the "chief learner" instead of the "General Manager."

Executive leaders build and sustain an environment where learning is supported and shared. Julie Tshida at Land O' Lakes and Brian McNulty at CDE provide examples of this type of leader in their organizations.

▲ It will not work without upper management support, period. People respond to what is asked of them. If you set an expectation for a 20% reduction in operating expenses, you will most likely see a 20% reduction. If upper management asks people, "What have you done to contribute to our effectiveness as the learning organization?" they're going to try to respond to that. (JT, LOL: 21)

▲ What I hope I bring is that I'm a good translator. I try to listen to what people say, then reframe it so that people can understand it. Because people tend to talk in the way that they think, we miss each other lots of times. . . . We have wonderfully creative, talented people. My job is to make sure that this is a creative work space so that they love working here. (BM, CDE: 152)

These kinds of leaders not only talk about the importance of learning, they also live it. It is important that employees routinely hear and see their leaders engaging in learning activities, talking with others about learning, and planning future learning initiatives. Leadership is not just telling people what is important and what to do. It is about consistently modeling the behaviors that leaders wish to see in their employees.

Leadership Within the Organization

For learning through evaluative inquiry to occur, leadership at all levels of the organization must support and implement it. Senge (1996) outlines various types of leaders necessary for building a learning organization. *Local line leaders* try out different organizational experiments to determine the extent to which the experiment can lead to improved business results. These people are department or unit heads, often responsible for the bottom-line results—and whose approval typically would be necessary for the use of time and resources on evaluative inquiry activities. Examples of this kind of leader are provided by three of our interviewees:

▲ My new supervisor has taken the learning organization on . . . he embraces the idea. So, he'll remind me often, "This isn't the type of thing where you have to go to your desk and solve the problem. Let's talk about it." (MB, Ford: 45)

▲ A manager does two things: Looks at tomorrow and then does a lot of investigation about what it's going to take to be successful in the new world. He then translates that back to determining where his people are and what they have to do next. (SS, LOL: 152)

▲ My unit director said, "If we're going to be a unit, we've got to decide what our purpose is." So he brought together the group with a facilitator and they hammered through—he's the kind of person who doesn't need a lot of control and was very willing to go with the team consensus model. They developed their priorities, they developed their mission statement, they developed their own name, and they developed how they were going to work together. (BM, CDE: 309)

Local line leaders become teachers, helping others understand the value of experimentation and the learning that results from such efforts. These leaders are often able to influence executive leaders to support evaluative inquiry efforts.

Internal networkers or *community builders* are what Senge calls the "seed carriers" of the learning culture. They move around the organization, much like a bee, pollinating learning in hosts who are receptive to organizational experiments and new learnings. David Berdish at Visteon, an enterprise of Ford Motor Company, calls these people "rebel leaders." He explains:

> These rebel grassroots leaders may never see a manager position at all, but know what the right thing to do is and they care a lot about their jobs. And that could be a guy on the floor, it could be a general salaried engineer. They just care about doing the best thing. (DB, Ford: 67)

Internal networkers are often invisible in the power structure—they come from all areas of the organization. Networkers seek out those who are open to developing new learning capabilities. Instead of trying to convince individuals who are resistant to the new learning culture, the internal networker builds on the interests and strengths of those who have the energy to change. They avoid cooptation and habitual responsiveness to management concerns by (a) understanding contextual influences on the practice and use of evaluative inquiry within the organization, (b) working to maximize trust and credibility with all constituents, (c) aligning inquiry methods with the epistemological orientations of others in the organization, (d) raising and representing issues to those in authority, (e) educating senior management on the relationship between their perspectives and the perspectives of others, and (f) maintaining a tolerance for ambiguity and incremental change (Torres, 1991). This approach contributes to building a critical mass that helps shift the organization's culture toward supporting inquiry and learning.

Leadership that supports inquiry and learning is needed at all levels in an organization and may take many different shapes. These kinds of leaders model the processes of evaluative inquiry, and they understand that without their leadership, systemic long-term change will never occur. They accept individual differences, are committed to the development of each member of the organization, have a tolerance for disagreement, and capitalize on people's openness. They ask good questions, are active listeners, and build on people's strengths to build community.

Fundamentally, they care about the people whom they employ. In one survey of *Fortune* 500 company executives, respondents cited compassion as one of the most important characteristics needed for success; only team building was mentioned more often. Belenky, Bond, and Weinstock (1997) liken effective leaders to midwife leaders because they "pull people into intense and continual discussions. They inspire everyone to question and construct views of how things *actually* work. They also encourage people to develop a vision of how things *ought* to work" (p. 14)—both of which are integral to evaluative inquiry.

COMMUNICATION

In most organizations today, there is an increasing amount of data being collected—from customers, clients, employees, consultants, and market researchers. The problem is not that there is not enough data with which to answer an organization's questions, but that the quality, timeliness, and content of existing data do not meet the information and learning needs of organization members. Nor is sufficient time typically devoted to meaningful interpretation of the data that are available. In addition, many organizations lack the necessary information systems and channels to ensure that those who need information can retrieve and make use of it quickly and easily. Such systems are often underutilized for several reasons: (a) Organization members are not aware of what data are available, (b) the systems do not collect relevant data and are not being maintained on a consistent basis, or (c) staff lack the technical expertise to generate reports that would make the data more accessible and useful to others in the organization.

How information is communicated to organization members and the organization's external constituents is a key determinant of the extent to which an organization wishes to learn (see Exhibit 7.3). Indeed, the entry point for any learning to occur is communication. It is difficult to think of anything more fundamental to establishing a learning community than communication. The efficacy of shared learning is often dependent on individuals' prior knowledge, the ways in which information is communicated, the extent to which members are experiencing information overload, and the need for individuals to unlearn or to discard previous knowledge (Huber, 1991).

Going back to the roadway system metaphor we used earlier, communication occurs via the roads, along which cognitive and affective data travel back and forth, and in and out of the organization. Evaluative inquiry itself is a major vehicle for organizational communication, providing a means for the expression of attitudes, feelings, intentions, and opposing views—which in turn contributes to new insights and mutual understanding.

Traditionally, evaluators have used a very narrow range of formats for communicating their activities and findings—that is, technical reports, executive summaries, and formal presentations delivered to the program managers and other organizational leaders (Torres et al., 1997). Many of these types of communications are "media-low" (Daft & Huber, 1987); that is, they are particularly "efficient for processing large amounts of objective data" (p. 20) but may not facilitate the understanding or interpretation of data. Information low in media richness takes more time to be understood and is generally less insightful.

On the other hand, a medium is considered rich if it provides insight and facilitates learning quickly. A rich communication transaction results in a major change in mental representation or how one thinks about the topic. Face-to-face and telephone communications are media rich because they allow for personal feedback and utilize natural language. Not surprisingly, practicing evaluators have reported that successful communications include vivid, concrete illustrations of findings that allow audiences to assimilate information quickly and easily—both positive and negative findings, and qualitative, contextual data. Successful communications also are interactive, allowing for early collaboration and involvement of stakeholders, especially in the interpretation of findings (Torres et al., 1997).

Effective communication of any kind within organizations is now also being challenged by the sheer volume of information available to us, the accessibility of which has been significantly increased by technological advances such as e-mail, the Internet, and fax machines. Stewart (1997) makes a distinction between information in organizations that is *pushed*

EXHIBIT 7.3.

Communication Within Organizations That Facilitates Evaluative Inquiry

- ▲ *Uses information for learning, not personal power*
- ▲ *Disseminates information that captures a diversity of voices*
- ▲ *Uses information as a means to share learning among co-workers*
- ▲ *Collects and makes available logistical data, as well as providing a means for interpreting data*
- ▲ *Uses technology to manage, disseminate, and increase access to information*
- ▲ *Eliminates structural barriers to face-to-face communications*

at us and information that we *pull* for ourselves. Information pushed at us includes documents we receive without requesting them, such as monthly budget figures, enrollment figures, sales numbers, test score reports, e-mail messages, minutes of meetings, and evaluation communications and reports. As we experience this kind of overload, we tend to ignore and not use a great deal of unsolicited information.

To the extent that evaluative inquiry is embedded in the ongoing routines of organizational practice, as opposed to the episodic nature of discrete evaluation studies, the resulting communications will be more useful for organizational learning. Relatedly, as a means of clearing the desk and cutting down on the amount of paper disseminated and eventually wasted, many organizations are developing technology systems that allow employees to access information they need when they need it. In past years, leaders rarely asked for information, but today, the majority of *Fortune* 500 companies are building internal systems that collect and disseminate all kinds of data useful for evaluative inquiry, as illustrated in the following examples.

- Honda distributes copies of its strategic plan to all employees.
- Marriott Hotels has a newsletter that contains a question and answer section from customers about excellent service.
- Microsoft has a "best practice" database that is used to share innovative ideas across units.
- Baxter Healthcare shares weekly cash flow information to all employees.
- The World Bank shares critical information via an on-line "kiosk."
- Federal Express reports daily activity statistics to all employees (Ashkenas et al., 1995, pp. 75-77).

Another example is Hewlett-Packard, where policies, telephone directories, product descriptions, and internal reports are provided on-line through the organization's intranet. Technology thus allows workers to *pull* information on a need-to-know basis. The result is a greater likelihood that information will be available when needed for ongoing evaluative inquiry efforts, while also eliminating the mountains of unwanted paper that all too quickly accumulates on one's desk, never to be read. These kinds of communication systems facilitated by technology are *logistical* to handle the *processing of data* (Daft & Huber, 1987). The learning processes and phases of evaluative inquiry, on the other hand, are *interpretive* communication systems because they facilitate the *understanding of data*.

Although many organizations are attempting to share information internally, others still restrict access to information to those in power, or have not yet developed effective dissemination systems. In many cases, individuals and teams have learned from a particular project or experience but have not had the means with which (or any incentive) to disseminate their learning. Shaw and Perkins (1991) call this "solution ignorance." This occurs when isolated groups identify problems and solutions but do not share their approaches with others in the organization. Failure to share in organizations occurs for several reasons. First, there may be real or perceived boundaries preventing group members from safely sharing their learning. Whether these boundaries result from internal politics, reward and incentive systems, or a belief that information is power not to be shared, people withhold their knowledge from others. Competition between employees also impedes the dissemination of knowledge. For example, if the organization's culture rewards individual achievements to the exclusion of team accomplishments, then information will be protected and guarded, not shared. Organizations that suppress information, that provide access only to those in powerful positions, and/or that manipulate and distort information do not act in ways that are consistent with organizational learning principles (Preskill, Lackey, & Caracelli, 1997). Interestingly, research has shown that employees' work satisfaction is highly correlated not only with high performance but also with high levels of communication (Buchholz, Roth, & Hess, 1987).

Ultimately, whatever types and modes of communication are established should be those that are easily accessible to organization members. When employees have restricted access to information, individual, team, and organizational learning will be limited. In addition, evaluative inquiry efforts will be impeded if information is not readily available for addressing questions the organization seeks to answer. Although it is likely that information always will be used by some as an instrument of power, information that results from evaluative inquiry should be conceived of and applied as a democratizing force. Within a supportive learning culture, information has the capacity to bring forth a diversity of voices that enriches employees' professional and personal development and growth.

SYSTEMS AND STRUCTURES

The systems and structures of an organization mediate organization members' ability to interact, collaborate, and communicate with each other—and thus, the success of evaluative inquiry efforts. (see Exhibit 7.4) Unfortunately, traditional organizational structures frequently have led to the fragmentation of work tasks and have contributed little to helping employees understand how what they do affects others' jobs. Many employees have functioned independently and have had little need or ability to link their efforts with others in the

EXHIBIT 7.4.

Organizational Systems and Structures That Facilitate Evaluative Inquiry

---

▲ *Support collaboration, communication, and cooperation among organization members as well as across units or departments*

▲ *Help organization members understand how their role relates to other roles in the organization and to the organization's mission as a whole*

▲ *Recognize individuals and their capacity to learn as the organization's greatest resource*

▲ *Value the whole person and support personal as well as professional development*

▲ *Use reward systems that recognize team as well as individual learning and performance*

---

organization. For example, if you were in marketing, you conversed and worked with people in marketing. If you were a fourth grade teacher, you may have talked primarily with other fourth grade teachers. Organizations have provided little incentive to collaborate across work units. As a result, the sharing of information and the development and flow of ideas throughout the organization have been constrained. In response to the limitations of the old structures and the needs of today's organizations, some suggest that the "best organizational structure is one that does not seem to exist: a transparent, superconducting connection between people and customers" (Stewart, 1997, p. 140). When an organization's structure is developed with a systems perspective, members come to understand how what they do contributes to other employees' work, and ultimately to the organization's success. As Ashkenas and colleagues (1995) explain:

No longer will organizations use boundaries to separate people, tasks, processes, and places; instead, they will focus on how to permeate those boundaries—to move ideas, information, decisions, talent, rewards, and actions where they are most needed. (p. 2)

Integrated systems and structures erase boundaries between departments and units, eliminate negative competition, and create opportunities for learning and knowledge dissemination. To illustrate the company's approach to applications software design, SAP America took out a clever full-page ad in *Fortune* magazine (February 5, 1996) that shows a man holding a black and white picture of a cow. The cow is partitioned into nine separate sections by dotted lines. The caption reads:

This is an organizational chart that shows the different parts of a cow. In a real cow, the parts are not aware that they're parts. They do not have trouble sharing information. They smoothly and naturally work together as one unit. As a cow. And you have only one question to answer. Do you want your company to work like a chart? Or a cow?

We think this metaphor makes clear how we have forgotten the importance and value of working together. A number of the organizations we studied echoed this notion. Dave Smith, a unit director at the Colorado Department of Education, describes the importance of integrating work functions and modeling teamwork for communities:

When I was doing work in dropout prevention, I was the only one actually assigned to that from the Department. I actually worked outside of the Department with another team of people who were employed by the University of Colorado and other agencies; so it was an interagency group. Part of what we found after a couple of years was that no one system could deal with this issue by itself—that we all had to figure out ways to work together. In making this recommendation to the State and to the General Assembly, we also took that recommendation to heart within the Department. We could no longer afford to have Safe and Drug Free Schools working in one part of the department and an HIV Aids initiative working in another part. We figured if we wanted to promote collaboration in communities, we needed to model it here within the Department. And so, under the belief that it takes people working in teams to address this issue, we pulled those initiatives together—so that we would model that from the very beginning by being a team. (DS, CDE: 244)

Brian Schatz, an administrative director with Presbyterian Healthcare Services, describes his organization's efforts toward integration and collaboration in the following way:

As an organization we are pursuing concepts of process management and trying to manage key processes across department and division lines as opposed to the old way we managed a department. You know: These are my people. Those are your people. I do this and then I pass it to you. (BS, Pres: 222)

Carolyn Thompson, Director of the Center for Organizational Learning at Presbyterian Hospital, relates learning to changes in organizational structure:

If we can go deeper and really begin to look at the patterns, then we begin to see that we have addressed this event many times before. . . . If we begin to understand the patterns, then we can begin to look at structure. What are the actual structural changes that we need to make so that whatever events-based management we have, makes some kind of sense. So I see this as very structural, as actually mucking—allowing people the opportunity to muck with the way they think about how the business is organized.

To identify and to use some quantum physics examples or Newtonian physics—we do not break things into tiny little parts and then put it back and understand how it works. This is a much more systemic process where we have to understand the whole, and the whole has to do with how I think and how that's different from the way you think. How the processes which made me successful yesterday may not serve me today

and tomorrow. And then making conscious decisions about what I can
do to shift those structures. (CT, Pres: 219)

Finally, Mary Vanderwall, a supervisor at the Colorado Department
of Education, describes how her view of being a learning organization
became more inclusive.

One thing that I never realized is how important the whole continuum
is. I think I considered organizational learning more like build[ing] a
library of books. To me I thought it was learning together. But now I can
see that it's a philosophy about everything we do from being hired and
the process that goes along with that, to how we go about our work
every day, how we relate to each other, how we're organized, and what
kind of team we're organized into. Just everything has to do with [being
a] learning organization. There's just nothing that should be left out. (MV,
CDE: 262)

In the remainder of this chapter, we describe two major interrelated
elements of an organization's systems and structures that can support
evaluative inquiry. They are job design and the role of human resource
development.

Job Design

Chapter 2 describes the role of teamwork in implementing evaluative
inquiry. Here we discuss how the use of teams, networking, and cross-
training for evaluative inquiry parallels many of the teamwork initiatives
already going on in organizations as they attempt to capitalize on
employees' intellectual capital. Many organizations are, and will be,
structuring their work processes in ways that bring employees together
to work on organizational issues. Team learning seeks to create "a shared
meaning about a process, a product, or an event" (Schrage, 1989, p. 33),
where individuals come to know themselves and each other better in
the process. In general, teamwork can be thought of as:

A continuous, strategically-used process that results in changes in knowledge, beliefs and behaviors. Learning takes place through the ongoing dialectical process of action and reflection as a collective discipline involving mastering the practices of dialogue and discussion. These are enacted through changes in policies, procedures, and systems. (Horvath, Callahan, Croswell, & Mukri, 1996, p. 417)

To facilitate and manage organizational change, organizations will be broken down into 2- to 50-member teams so that they may be more efficient in their learning, will accomplish work through project teams that may have lives of a few hours to many weeks and months, will develop shorter feedback loops, will use peer evaluations more than supervisor or manager evaluations, and will require real-time access to all information for all organization members (Peters, 1992).

Further evidence of the trend toward using teams is reported in the "Training Magazine Industry Report" (1994), which found that in organizations with more than 100 employees, 73% were members of a working group identified as a "team" (p. 62). In "Training Magazine Industry Report" (1997), 41% of the survey respondents said that one of their current workplace initiatives was making the "transition to teams-based structure" (p. 62). The 1997 survey also reports that 75% of the responding organizations provide training on "Team Building" (p. 55). Job design that allows for teamwork, networking across projects, and cross-training facilitates the successful implementation of evaluative inquiry.

At Xerox, management's support of team autonomy and innovation has been associated with decreased absenteeism and improved customer responsiveness (Martinez, 1997). When managers began shifting the corporate culture away from one dominated by control, they instructed teams to develop their own approaches to improving business results and employee satisfaction. As a result, teams developed a multitude of work schedules that better fit the business and personal needs of employees.

Another example of collaboration and communication designed to increase learning is seen in how the Colorado Department of Education explicitly promotes networking across state-funded local educational

improvement projects (school districts and consortia). Grantees participate in three 1-day meetings throughout the funding cycle to discuss
current implementation issues, dissemination, evaluation of their projects, and other technical assistance. On one recent networking day, they
used "tuning protocols" to present implementation issues related to
their projects and receive feedback from a supportive, problem-solving
group of other grantees. To stimulate further networking, grantees also
visit at least one other site during the school year.

Initiated originally to provide employees greater flexibility in their
work options, job sharing and cross-training are other means of promoting collaboration and communication within organizations. Successful
job-sharing arrangements dependent on creative thinking, strong communication skills, trust between job sharers and managers, commitment, and compromise (Sheley, 1996). Cross-training helps ensure that
employees understand all aspects of the organization's functioning, a
valuable asset for members of an evaluative inquiry team. Many predict
that in the future, the value of the sum of a person's work experience
will be in the number of roles one has played in a number of organizations, not the titles a person has held.

> Successful participation requires everyone to have a basic under-
> standing of the business and industry, the organization's paying
> customers, the key forces shaping the organization, and the gen-
> eral functions of the groups that work in and with it. Such a broad
> business and cross-functional understanding helps people, no
> matter what their role, to see themselves in the larger context and
> subject to the interdependencies of the business. It gives them the
> meaning and perspective that enable them to make good decisions
> about what to do and whom to involve, whatever the problem or
> situation. (McLagan & Nel, 1995, p. 146)

Relatedly, team-based evaluation and reward systems are being designed to rekindle interest in performance for its own sake, as well as to
link that performance to the mission and vision of the organization.
Compensation based on group performance can occur at the project
team and/or departmental or unit levels. For example, project team

members might receive a bonus by sharing in estimated savings when important targets are met, or merit pay might be based on the effectiveness of a total unit as reflected by a unitwide performance appraisal (Harrington-Mackin, 1994). These practices de-emphasize individual performance and competitiveness, and encourage team or unit members to focus on the collective effect of their work. According to Daniel Burnham, president of Allied-Signal, "the signs of career progress are the richness of your work's content and the size of its impact on the organization" (cited in Stewart, 1997, p. 206). Clearly, significant organizational impact cannot be achieved by individuals alone.

It is through teams that learning from evaluative inquiry is most effectively shared throughout the organization; "what is learned impacts the organization as a whole. It is embedded in the way the organization does its business and is shared throughout the organization, even though this may not be always conscious" (Watkins & Marsick, 1993, p. 156). Team-based job design will be the primary mechanism for helping organizations adapt to the continuing challenges and changes described in Chapter 1. Ultimately, teams represent work groups made up of individuals who are interdependent because of the work tasks they perform within a larger social system (e.g., schools, businesses, nonprofit organizations, communities) (Guzzo & Dickson, 1996). Evaluative inquiry team members understand that the effects of their work are maximized when they share knowledge and create new meanings through their collaborative efforts. Team learning enables individuals to make better decisions, develop increased confidence in their subsequent actions, and develop greater buy-in and active commitment to the organization's goals for evaluative inquiry.

The Changing Role of Human Resource Development

As organizations are looking more like composites of mutually interdependent parts functioning together, the role of human resource development (HRD) within organizations is having to shift its focus. This change in HRD's role is well documented (see Bassi & Van Buren, 1998;

Davis & Mink, 1992; Dixon, 1992, 1994; Preskill, 1997; Watkins & Marsick, 1992). The HRD function is becoming more organic than mechanistic as it moves toward fostering self-organization, creativity, systems thinking, and teamwork. Jack Martin, Vice-President of Human Resources at Land O' Lakes, explained HRD's changing role in his organization:

The role of HR at Land O' Lakes has changed quite a bit. It's kind of moved over the years from policy and administration to strategic issues related to human resources. We're out of the administration and policy development business, and we're into consulting on issues of organization and employee development, and working on major organizational development initiatives throughout our system. . . . We've eliminated training and development as a corporate function. Training is part of the overall learning system. . . . [We] help our intellectual assets be the best they can be. (JM, LOL: 189, 191)

Through these kinds of shifts, HRD is more solidly positioned to support evaluative inquiry efforts within organizations. That is, in organizations working to establish a learning culture, trainers and HRD specialists are more likely to be functioning as internal consultants with a variety of roles that facilitate learning at all levels within the organization. These include

- Brokering and facilitating learning services rather than delivering stand-up training
- Focusing on performance improvement and problem solving
- Facilitating communication within the organization

Sharon Stone, a quality process consultant at Land O' Lakes, explained, "The training and development area has more or less been disbanded as an HR function and put back into the organization" (SS, LOL: 147). Direct delivery of training to employees is more likely to be seen among line managers and supervisors who are adopting more of a coaching and mentoring role with subordinates (Fenman, Ltd., 1996;

"Training Magazine Industry Report," 1997). McLagan and Nel (1995) claim, "Everyone in a participative organization must develop at least a basic level of skills in these helping functions. If they do not, they cannot pass their knowledge capital on to others, and they cannot help others grow" (p. 153). Carolyn Thompson, Director of Organizational Learning at Presbyterian Hospital, explained her experience in helping a colleague learn and grow through a mentoring relationship:

> The medical director of one of our programs became extremely interested in organizational learning. He came to me and said "Will you mentor me?" and I was able to mentor him and he actually helped to facilitate one of our leadership projects. So I got to support him and he was in the main facilitator role. We would have never known that interest existed. And now he's back in full-time practice as a physician and is using those tools and techniques, as well as what he learned through that process working with his own group, his own practice. So, there was incredible cross-functionality and the connects were just amazing. (CT, Pres: 202)

Self-managed learning is another recurring theme in employee learning and development. Those serious about their own professional development are advised to approach it proactively (Peterson & Hicks, 1997) by (a) focusing on situations with high potential for change and where the employee controls the outcome, but is forced to think in new ways; (b) stepping back from their work to view issues from others' perspectives; (c) getting involved in cross-functional or interdepartmental activities; and (d) taking intelligent risks to foster the learning that occurs at the boundary between stretching limits and going over the edge.

Finally, effective HRD units are beginning to view all workers as knowledge workers. In the coming years, power in organizations is likely to come from expertise, not from position (Stewart, 1997). Workers play a variety of roles—fact finder, interpreter, diagnostician, judge, adjuster, and change agent (Trist, 1981). The need for the kinds of process skills these roles require is increasingly being recognized within U.S. organizations. Respondents to a survey conducted by ASTD (1996a) report that employers are primarily looking for applicants with listening and oral communication skills (75%), problem-solving skills (60%), and interpersonal skills (54%).

The notion of organizational members as knowledge workers provides a humanistic perspective as the basis for hiring, retaining, and promoting individuals (Jenlink & Torres, 1995). This view assumes that:

- People are curious, intellectually able, and inventive
- At the heart . . . of the learning organization is learners' ability and willingness to transcend conventional work-life boundaries
- Knowledge workers can and should be partners in determining their own learning—they must be both co-producers and co-consumers of their learning as their work
- Knowledge workers are professionals who have sufficient knowledge, skill, and experience in common to promote important collegial learning
- Knowledge workers' life interests are comprehensive and integrated with their work—even when those interests may appear to be distinct from the content of their work (p. 157)

Mary Vanderwall, a supervisor at the Colorado Department of Education, reflected on this more balanced view of personal and professional life for employees:

I also have a strong belief about bringing personal goals into work. I learned this lesson from a supervisor I had when I began here. On a yearly basis, he used a form that included personal and professional goals. I had never been encouraged to bring my personal life into my professional life. In fact, it was a taboo, you just didn't do it. Going through that process even though it only was once a year, made me realize the importance. We are who we are and it all goes together. If we don't recognize that, we're not only missing the boat, but missing an opportunity to build on personal strengths. So I really do like to pay attention to this. Obviously, that could go to the extreme and be very unhealthy.

> There has to be balance. But to set professional goals totally separate from personal goals doesn't work very well. (MV, CDE: 260)

As Sergiovanni (1994) explains:

> Becoming a community of learners . . . is an adventure not only in learning but an adventure in shared leadership and authentic relationships. It requires a certain equality and a certain willingness to know thyself better, to be open to new ideas, and to strive to become. It is an adventure in personal development. (p. 155)

This chapter has reviewed four components of an organization's infrastructure: its culture, leadership, communication, and systems and structures. These components will facilitate or inhibit organizational learning to varying degrees, depending on how they operate within the organization. First, in a learning organization, the culture encourages and supports continuous learning of all its employees, providing supportive environments where risks are taken without fear of failure or punishment, and employees trust one another. Second, leaders communicate their commitment to learning through their actions and by communicating a clear and practical learning vision. Third, the organization's communication system provides employees with channels and opportunities to access and share information as they need it. Fourth, integrated systems and structures within the organization facilitate organization-wide communication and collaboration and support learning at the individual, team, and organizational levels. In Chapter 8, we discuss how an evaluative inquiry team can overcome challenges presented when elements of their organization's infrastructure only partially support and facilitate the inquiry effort.

The Practice of
Evaluative Inquiry

R eaders familiar with the evaluation literature and field may be asking "How is evaluative inquiry for learning in organizations different from other collaborative, participatory, empowerment, or developmental approaches to evaluation?" This is a fair question. We believe that to varying degrees, each of these evaluation approaches positions the evaluator as a facilitator of learning in which stakeholders and program participants learn about themselves, each other, and the program through their involvement in the evaluation process (Brunner & Guzman, 1989; Cousins & Earl, 1992, 1995; Greene, 1988; Patton, 1994, 1997; Shapiro, 1988).

Whereas empowerment evaluation is more rooted in the politics of liberation and self-determination (Fetterman, 1994, 1996) than are participatory, collaborative, or developmental forms of evaluation, all four approaches emphasize learning as an outcome of the process, in addition to the more summative, product-oriented outcomes normally expected of an evaluation study. In this context, the evaluator seeks to teach clients and stakeholders evaluation skills and processes so that they may continue to engage in evaluation practice when the evaluator has left the scene.

Although evaluative inquiry for learning in organizations clearly overlaps with these other types of evaluation (as well as some organization development approaches), we believe that it also embodies at least four distinguishing characteristics. *First,* evaluative inquiry is integrated into the organization's work processes and is performed primarily by organization members. It is not something that is handed off to external consultants who are to figure out the problem and tell the organization what to do. Instead, trained evaluators (either internal or external) teach organization members the knowledge and skills of evaluative inquiry, and facilitate and model various inquiry processes.

Second, evaluative inquiry for organizational learning and change is ongoing; it is not episodic or event-driven, as are many evaluations and organization development interventions. Rather, it is used to nourish continuous individual, team, and organizational learning. Traditional evaluation and organization development efforts often are initiated when the organization perceives the existence of a serious problem or concern. Such events trigger some kind of inquiry and change, frequently facilitated by an external consultant or an internal department unconnected with the area in which the inquiry is focused.

Figure 8.1 compares evaluative inquiry and organization development. The horizontal line in the stepped graphic depicting organization development indicates the stable functioning of the organization. The point at which the line begins to show upward movement is when the results of the effort become available and are used to make improvements. Over time, however, the change has a plateauing effect, and things remain stable until the next crisis or problem surfaces. Once again, the consultant arrives to figure out the problem and, after some kind of intervention, makes recommendations on which additional changes are made. This approach is event-oriented, is reactive, and principally relies on outside knowledge to "fix" the problem.

Evaluative inquiry, on the other hand, is quite different. As shown in Figure 8.1, inquiry is not linear or episodic. Instead, learning as depicted by the upward spiral is continual and circular, feeding on itself to create

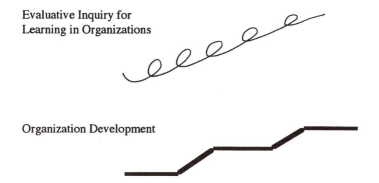

Evaluative Inquiry for
Learning in Organizations

Organization Development

Figure 8.1. Evaluative Inquiry Compared With Organization Development

new and higher forms of learning in the organization. It is both iterative and self-renewing. Evaluative inquiry is also about creating a community of inquirers who use inquiry skills on a daily basis to understand and improve organizational processes and systems. It is often initiated and facilitated by internal organization members closest to the problem or issue, and may rely on consultants to guide and teach about evaluative inquiry and provide technical assistance in evaluation and research methods as needed.

Third, evaluative inquiry for learning in organizations strongly relies on the democratic processes of asking questions and exploring individuals' values, beliefs, assumptions, and knowledge through dialogue and reflection. It seeks to include a diversity of voices. It is committed to the belief that varying viewpoints enrich both the process and the outcomes of the inquiry.

Fourth, evaluative inquiry contributes to a culture of inquiry and occurs within an infrastructure that values continuous improvement and learning. In this sense, it is culture-bound. Evaluative inquiry becomes embedded in organizational practices. Its processes and findings nourish the development of interpersonal and professional relationships, and strengthen organizational decision making.

EVALUATOR ROLES

Although there is a still a place for professional evaluators in this reconceptualization, the evaluator here, whether internal or external, is a collaborator, facilitator, interpreter, mediator, coach, and educator of learning and change processes. She may aid in getting the process going initially, but in some cases she intervenes thereafter only periodically to keep people actively involved in the inquiry process. Whether an evaluator is internal or external to the organization, her role is to facilitate dialogue and reflection through asking questions and identifying and clarifying organization members' values, beliefs, assumptions, and knowledge as they engage in each phase of the inquiry.

The evaluator encourages all voices to be heard and holds individuals accountable for any behaviors that discourage growth and action during the evaluative inquiry process. Thus, the evaluator is responsible for maintaining a climate that supports a spirit of inquiry, reciprocity, and community. In short, the evaluator's role is to model the learning processes of evaluative inquiry and to help people acquire and practice them. Finally, the evaluator works with stakeholders and program participants (1) to collaboratively determine the strengths and weaknesses of various organization programs, services, products, practices, processes, and systems, so that the organization may grow and develop; and (2) to maintain a climate that supports the continuous learning of all employees.

IMPLEMENTING EVALUATIVE
INQUIRY IN TODAY'S ORGANIZATIONS

Even for those of us who firmly believe that the approach to organizational learning we have described in this book is the most appropriate for organizations, we fully realize the numerous and formidable challenges we may face in instituting evaluative inquiry as part of our work practices. All organizations, however, are in a process of becoming—they are constantly evolving. It is highly unlikely that we will find any one organization where all the infrastructure components described in Chapter 7 are fully positioned to support evaluative inquiry. In many cases, the challenges we face relate to the organization not fully accepting and embracing the role of learning. In other cases, organizations lack an understanding of how to implement processes that support learning from inquiry. Some examples of these challenges, as discussed in Chapter 7, include the following.

- An anti-learning organizational culture exists, one that is reactive, not proactive.
- Leadership talks learning but does not model learning.
- Communication channels and systems are underdeveloped or underutilized to support organizational learning.
- Information is not willingly shared; the organization holds onto a belief that information is power.
- Dialogue and asking questions are not valued.
- Organization members do not generally trust one another.
- There is a fear of making mistakes; risk taking is avoided.
- Independent work is more highly valued than collaborative work.
- Evaluative activity is seen as threatening the status quo.
- Evaluative activity is seen as an "event."
- The diversity of stakeholders appears to be overwhelming.
- Evaluative activity is seen as costing too much in terms of money, time, and/or personnel resources.
- A general fear of change permeates the organization.
- People are suspicious of any data collection effort.

How then, can practitioners and consultants work within organizations to change the culture, to help establish the means and knowledge for evaluative inquiry? Our first task is to help organization members understand the components of their organization's infrastructure and their impact on evaluative inquiry and organizational learning efforts. For instance, we may need to help the organization's leadership understand that its present reward system is unlikely to support risk taking, and/or that the organization's present styles and methods of communication do not encourage collaboration among employees.

It is not so much that all the infrastructure elements must be in place and operating as described here for evaluative inquiry to succeed. Instead, as shown in Chapters 4-6, evaluative inquiry itself serves as a major vehicle for increasing understanding within organizations and as a catalyst for organizational change. The following strategies are not quick-fix solutions to the challenges cited above—systemic organizational change often takes at least 5 to 10 years to occur. These methods, however, will support incremental but substantive movement toward shaping a culture of inquiry and learning.

- Start with small inquiry projects before tackling larger issues.
- Invite people who you know are supportive of learning and willing to share their learning—do not try to convert everyone at once.
- Include as many diverse viewpoints as possible in each inquiry effort and value their involvement by listening and considering what they have to offer.
- Provide informal training to organization members on evaluative inquiry skills.
- Inform organizational leaders (at all levels) about your efforts—provide ongoing feedback about the inquiry's progress and results.
- Ask organization members what the costs are of not evaluating their efforts.
- In every situation, model the four learning processes (dialogue, reflection, asking questions, and identifying and clarifying values, beliefs, assumptions, and knowledge).
- Continually seek feedback on how the inquiry is progressing.
- Always emphasize the importance of the use of evaluative inquiry processes and findings. "What have we learned?" "What do we do now?" "Did our actions make a difference?"
- Publicize and celebrate the application of learning—let others know what you did, how you did it, and what has happened as a result.

OUTCOMES OF INDIVIDUAL, TEAM, AND ORGANIZATIONAL LEARNING

From our research and reading of the literature, we believe that evaluative inquiry for learning in organizations can contribute significantly to individual, team, and organizational learning. Its impacts can be described as both instrumental and conceptual in nature. Instrumental outcomes are usually pragmatic and reflect changes in the organization's structures, systems, products, services, or processes. They also may be related to individual and team performance where individuals and teams use information to solve problems, improve how their work is managed and organized, and find more effective methods for accomplishing their work. These outcomes are often tangible and measured through quantitative methods.

Conceptual outcomes reflect changes in individuals' growth and development with respect to how they think, feel, and act in the work environment. These outcomes are more incremental and are a product of the interactions between individuals and their engagement in the organizational learning process. Such changes may enhance individual self-esteem, promote better communication, bring people closer together, and result in organization members' willingness to take greater risks. An example of this type of change is provided by Krista Schulte at Ford Motor Company:

> One of the most important things is that it [becoming a learning organization] has created stronger bonds between the people. There's less of that feeling of isolation—of "I'm in this all by myself and the ship is going down, and my life's so hard." There's much more of a team sense that "we're in this together, and if I'm having trouble, I know other people I can go to for help." There's very much a sense of extended family in a way. (KS, Ford: 35)

Conceptual outcomes usually are less tangible, need more time to take effect before being measured, and are often obtained through

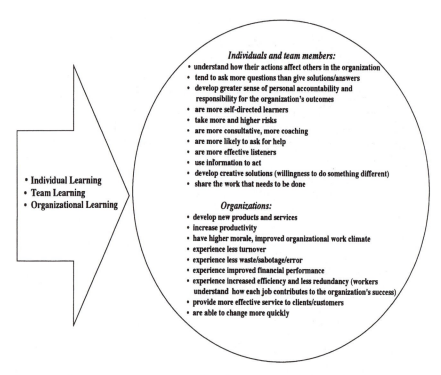

Figure 8.2. Outcomes Associated With Evaluative Inquiry For Learning

qualitative data collection methods. Although these outcomes can be maximized through evaluative inquiry, an organization must develop and maintain a supportive learning infrastructure (Chapter 7) for organization-wide learning to take place.

In spite of the potential benefits of evaluative inquiry, it is important not to overstate the promise of these outcomes, but instead to communicate the potential limitations of inquiry efforts in organizations that do not have supportive infrastructures. The path of change is likely to be bumpier and more incremental in such organizations. The spirit of this seemingly sober position is to meet organizations where they are and work to facilitate organizational learning accordingly. Doing so likely will mean spending considerable time at the outset on (a) relationship building and determining who to enlist to gain leadership support, and (b) clarifying issues and questions.

OUR HOPES

Our purpose for writing this book was to offer organization members, evaluators, and organizational development and management consultants another way of conceptualizing their practice. In particular, we believe that evaluative inquiry can be conceived of as a form of organizational learning that contributes to individual and team growth and development. Through dialogue and reflection, and through asking questions and identifying and clarifying values, beliefs, assumptions, and knowledge, organization members and the organization can learn from their practices and experiences to create a better future.

Although we acknowledge the idealism our approach embodies, we believe that without such aspirations, we are destined to make the same mistakes over and over again. We believe, therefore, that evaluative inquiry can be its own reward—it can be intrinsically satisfying and integral to an organization's community. What Robert Inchausti (1993) has said about teaching is also true of evaluative inquiry: It is impossible work. We never get it right; we always fall short of our high ideals. But we keep trying because, even with all its flaws and all its dangers, it remains our greatest hope for achieving communities of learning founded on mutual growth and shared understanding. We invite readers to join us on this journey and become champions of inquiry and learning in their organizations. As hard as it may be, and as discouraging as many days may seem, the potential, if the effort is successful, is a new kind of work environment that is ever more healthy and humane.

Questions for Facilitating Evaluative Inquiry

Defining the Evaluative Issue

4.1 What is the history or background of the problem/issue?

4.2 Have any previous inquiries been conducted regarding this topic? If yes, what were the results? How were the findings used?

4.3 Why is it important that we develop new insights into this problem/issue at this time?

4.4 What kinds of decisions would we like to make about the problem/issue?

4.5 What do we know about this problem/issue? What don't we know?

4.6 What organizational activities, procedures, or policies are part of the issue/problem?

4.7 What are the organizational variables that are affecting the context of the problem/issue?

4.8 What organizational politics are affecting the problem/issue?

4.9 What are our worst fears about this evaluative inquiry effort?

4.10 What are our hopes for what this evaluative inquiry effort will accomplish?

4.11 What is the purpose of the evaluative inquiry?

Identifying Stakeholders

4.12 What individuals or groups were mentioned as we worked to define the issues for this inquiry? What is their involvement with the problem/issue?

4.13 Why do we believe that each of these individuals or groups are stakeholders?

4.14 How might each of these individuals or groups be affected by the outcomes of this inquiry?

4.15 Which individuals or groups might use the findings for policy-making decisions?

4.16 Which individuals or groups might use the findings for making operational decisions?

4.17 Which individuals or groups might be interested in the findings but are not in a decision-making position relative to the subject of the inquiry?

4.18 Who has a "right to know" about the inquiry's findings?

4.19 Which of these individuals or groups should be involved in the process of the inquiry but are not currently on the inquiry team?

Determining Evaluative Questions

4.20 What questions should the inquiry seek to answer?

4.21 Why are these evaluative questions important?

4.22 What must we know now, versus what can we wait to know?

4.23 Which are the most critical questions?

4.24 What are the consequences if we do not answer these questions soon?

4.25 What do we hope will happen by answering these questions?

4.26 What do we think will happen if the answers to these questions are not in line with what certain stakeholders believe is true?

CHAPTER 5: CARRYING OUT THE INQUIRY

Designing the Inquiry

5.1 What kinds of data does the organization typically respond to? What does it ignore?

5.2 To what extent was the type of data from previous studies considered credible by the organization?

5.3 What are the preferred methods of those responsible for carrying out the data collection and analysis activities for the present inquiry?

5.4 What "political" issues related to the use of different data collection methods have surfaced in the past?

5.5 How might the answers to any of these questions influence decisions about the present inquiry?

Methods and Procedures for Data Collection

5.6 What kinds of data can best answer the evaluative inquiry questions we seek to answer?

5.7 What type of data will indicate if the activities, procedures, or policies in question are being implemented as intended or will inform us of any unanticipated outcomes?

5.8 What type of data will indicate if the intended outcomes of these activities, procedures, or policies in question are being realized?

5.9 What data already exist that might address the evaluative inquiry questions? Where does this information reside?

5.10 What other kinds of data (e.g., background information) might be available that would address the evaluative inquiry questions?

5.11 Will data be needed on an ongoing basis, or is the need more episodic—that is, particular to a one-time situation?

5.12 What logistical constraints (methodological, time, resources) must be considered?

5.13 What resources (technical/computer expertise, expenses, equipment, personnel time, access to particular personnel, etc.) will be needed to implement each data collection activity?

Methods and Procedures for
Data Analysis and Interpretation

5.14 How will each type of data collected be analyzed?

5.15 What expertise/resources will be needed? How much time will it take to analyze the data from each method used?

5.16 In what ways can different individuals and groups contribute to the analysis and interpretation of data?

Methods and Procedures for
Communicating and Reporting

5.17 What are some different analytic or reporting frameworks that might be appropriate for representing findings from the evaluative inquiry (e.g., the original evaluative questions, some organizational or programmatic framework, a new issues-oriented framework determined by the content of the findings)?

5.18 What does each stakeholder group need to know about how the inquiry is progressing and when? What is the best format and channel for communicating this information?

5.19 In addition to the previously identified stakeholders, who else should receive communications about the inquiry?

5.20 Is a comprehensive final report necessary? Will more informal reporting suffice?

Implementing Data Collection Efforts

5.21 Is the data collection plan being implemented as specified? If not, why not?

5.22 What new developments threaten successful implementation of the data collection activities?

5.23 How is the organization reacting to carrying out the inquiry?

5.24 What adjustments to the data collection plan need to be made?

5.25 What assumptions, values, beliefs, assumptions, and knowledge are proposed adjustments to the plan based upon?

5.26 What individuals or groups need to be apprised of adjustments made to the data collection plan?

Data Analysis and Interpretation

5.27 Are analysis and interpretation activities on schedule?

5.28 Do any new developments from either within or outside the organization threaten successful implementation of analysis and interpretation activities?

5.29 What adjustments to the analysis strategies are necessary? What individuals or groups need to be apprised of these adjustments?

5.30 How well does each possible different framework meet the learning needs of the organization?

5.31 What values, beliefs, assumptions, and knowledge are reflected in the choice of a particular analytic or reporting framework?

5.32 What other perspectives should be considered?

5.33 How should quantitative and qualitative data be presented?

5.34 How should data across departments or sites be integrated and presented?

Developing Recommendations

5.35 What evidence supports each recommendation?

5.36 Does the set of recommendations represent all findings of the inquiry?

5.37 Do recommendations take into account what is known about organizational context, logistics, and constraints?

5.38 What particular values, beliefs, or assumptions are reflected in each recommendation?

Communicating and Reporting

5.39 Are communications and reports written in a clear, jargon-free style?

5.40 Have tables and figures been used effectively to make information more understandable?

5.41 Has the communication of negative findings been handled productively (e.g., within the context of continuous improvement and learning)?

5.42 Have findings and interpretations been appropriately summarized for different audiences?

5.43 Does the format of each communication/report facilitate easy interpretation and assimilation of its content?

CHAPTER 6: APPLYING LEARNING

Identifying and Selecting Action Alternatives

6.1 What priority should each recommendation be given (low, medium, high)?

6.2 What reasoning is behind each prioritization?

6.3 What values, beliefs, assumptions, and knowledge are reflected in reasons given?

6.4 In what possible (additional) ways can this recommendation be addressed?

6.5 Specifically, what will this action alternative achieve?

6.6 What groups and individuals would be involved in the implementation of this action alternative?

6.7 What other groups and individuals will be affected by it?

6.8 What are potential undesirable consequences of this alternative?

6.9 How much will implementation of this action cost? What other resources will it require?

6.10 What new skills, knowledge, and attitudes will organizational members need to acquire to facilitate this action's success?

6.11 What incentives are there for organizational members to make the changes in their daily practices that it will require?

6.12 To what extent will the organization's existing infrastructure (culture, leadership, modes of communication, other systems and structures) either support or undermine implementation of this action alternative?

6.13 Conversely, what impact will it likely have on any elements of the infrastructure?

6.14 In what groups, teams, departments, and/or individuals is this action alternative likely to be met with resistance?

6.15 What additional obstacles or barriers, if any, might impede successful implementation? What could be done to overcome any of these barriers?

6.16 What has been the organization's experiences with similar change initiatives?

Developing an Action Plan

6.17 What steps are necessary to carry out this action alternative? Are there several broad categories of action, each of which has smaller substeps?

6.18 How will the critical issues for successful implementation (outlined in the previous phase of identifying and selecting the action alternative) be accounted for in these steps?

6.19 Who should be responsible for carrying out each step/substep?

6.20 What amount of time realistically will be required to do so?

6.21 Are there critical organizational events that must be accounted for in developing the timeline for implementation?

6.22 How will we know if the action is being implemented successfully?

6.23 At what point(s) should dialogues to monitor progress take place?

6.24 Who should be involved in these dialogues?

Implementing the Action Plan and Monitoring Progress

6.25 How is actual implementation paralleling intended implementation, and what can we learn from any discrepancies?

6.26 What new issues are surfacing that impact the success of the change being made?

6.27 What adjustments to the plan are necessary, and what is the best way to make them?

6.28 What barriers or obstacles are impeding full implementation?

References

Allee, V. (1997). 12 principles of knowledge management. *Training & Development,* *51*(11), 71-74.

Allerton, H. (1996). A different sort of corporate merger. *Training & Development,* *50*(6), 8.

American Society for Training and Development. (1996a). Basic skills 1996 survey results. *Survey 2, 1996.* Alexandria, VA: Author.

American Society for Training and Development. (1996b). Building a learning organization. *Survey 3, 1996.* Alexandria, VA: Author.

American Society for Training and Development. (1996c). Leadership development 1996 survey results. *Survey 1, 1996.* Alexandria, VA: Author.

American Society for Training and Development. (1997). Intellectual capital. *Survey 1, 1997.* Alexandria, VA: Author.

Argyris, C. (1985). *Strategy, change and defensive routines.* Marshfield, MA: Pitman.

Argyris, C. (1992). *On organizational learning.* Cambridge, MA: Blackwell Business.

Argyris, C., & Schon, D. A. (1978). *Organizational learning: A theory of action perspective.* Reading, MA: Addison-Wesley.

Argyris, C., & Schon, D. A. (1996). *Organizational learning II: Theory, method and practice.* Reading, MA: Addison-Wesley.

Ashkenas, R., Ulrich, D., Jick, T., & Kerr, S. (1995). *The boundaryless organization: Breaking the chains of organizational structure.* San Francisco: Jossey-Bass.

B. F. [Bob Filipczak]. (1994). The change monster. *Training, 31*(5), 136.

Barrett, F. J. (1995). Creating appreciative learning cultures. *Organizational Dynamics, 24*(2), 36-48.

Bart, C. K. (1998, January 7). Second World Congress on the Management of Intellectual Capital. (Available through e-mail at orgcult@commerce.uq.edu.au)

Bassi, L. J., & Van Buren, M. E. (1998). *The 1998 ASTD state of the industry report.* Alexandria, VA: American Society for Training and Development.

Bateson, G. (1972). *Steps to an ecology of mind.* New York: Ballantine.

Belenky, M. F., Bond, L. A., & Weinstock, J. S. (1997). *A tradition that has no name.* New York: Basic Books.

Binns, P. (1994). Organisations: Valuing and learning. In J. G. Burgoyne, M. Pedler, & T. Boydell (Eds.), *Toward the learning company: Concepts and practices.* Maidenhead, UK: McGraw-Hill.

Bohm, D. (1996). *On dialogue* (L. Nichol, Ed.). London: Routledge.

Bourque, L. B., & Fielder, E. P. (1995). *How to conduct self-administered and mail surveys.* Thousand Oaks, CA: Sage.

Brache, A. P., & Rummler, G. A. (1997). Managing an organization as a system. *Training, 34*(2), 68-74.

Brinkerhoff, R. O. (1989). *Achieving results from training.* San Francisco: Jossey-Bass.

Brookfield, S. D. (1995). *Becoming a critically reflective teacher.* San Francisco: Jossey-Bass.

Brookfield, S. D., & Preskill, S. L. (1998). *Talking democratically.* San Francisco: Jossey-Bass.

Brooks, A. K. (1994). Power and production of knowledge: Collective team learning in work organizations. *Human Resource Development Quarterly, 5*(3), 213-235.

Brooks, A., & Watkins, K. E. (Eds.). (1994). The emerging power of action inquiry technologies [Special issue]. *New Directions for Adult and Continuing Education, 63*(Fall).

Brown, J. (1995). Dialogue: Capacities and stories. In S. Chawla & J. Renesch (Eds.), *Learning organizations: Developing cultures for tomorrow's workplace* (pp. 153-164). Portland, OR: Productivity Press.

Brunner, I., & Guzman, A. (1989). Participatory evaluation: A tool to assess projects and empower people. *New Directions in Program Evaluation, 42*, 9-17.

Bryner, A., & Markova, D. (1996). *An unused intelligence.* Berkeley, CA: Canari.

Buchholz, S., Roth, T., & Hess, K. (1987). *Creating the high-performance team.* New York: John Wiley & Sons.

Burgoyne, J. G. (1992). Creating a learning organization. *Royal Society for the Arts Journal, 140*(5428), 321-332.

Canning, C. (1991). What teachers say about reflection. *Educational Leadership, 49*(3), 18-21.

Carleton, J. R. (1997). Cultural due diligence. *Training, 34*(11), 67-75.

Chalofsky, N. (1996). A new paradigm for learning in organizations. *Human Resource Development Quarterly, 7*(3), 287-293.

Chawla, S. (1995). Conclusion: Reflections of learning from a gathering. In S. Chawla & J. Renesch (Eds.), *Learning organizations: Developing cultures for tomorrow's workplace* (pp. 501-508). Portland, OR: Productivity Press.

Chawla, S., & Renesch, J. (Eds.). (1995). *Learning organizations: Developing cultures for tomorrow's workplace.* Portland, OR: Productivity Press.

Clark, J., & Koonce, R. (1995). Meetings go high-tech. *Training & Development, 49*(11), 32-38.

Coffey, A., & Atkinson, P. (1996). *Making sense of qualitative data: Complementary research practices.* Thousand Oaks, CA: Sage.

Cohen, M. D., & Sproull, L. S. (Eds.). (1996). *Organizational learning.* Thousand Oaks, CA: Sage.

Cousins, J. B., & Earl, L. M. (1992). The case for participatory evaluation. *Educational Evaluation and Policy Analysis, 14*(4), 397-418.

Cousins, J. B., & Earl, L. M. (1995). The case for participatory evaluation: Theory, research, practice. In J. B. Cousins & L. M. Earl (Eds.), *Participatory evaluation in education* (pp. 5-18). London: Falmer.

Cranton, P. (1994). *Understanding and promoting transformative learning.* San Francisco: Jossey-Bass.

Cunningham, J. B. (1993). *Action research and organizational development.* Westport, CT: Praeger.

Daft, R. L., & Huber, G. P. (1987). How organizations learn: A communication framework. *Research in the Sociology of Organizations, 5*, 1-36.

Davis, L. N., & Mink, O. G. (1992). Human resource development: An emerging profession—an emerging purpose. *Studies in Continuing Education, 14*(2), 187-204.

Davis, S. (1996). Rumble, rumble. *Training & Development, 50*(11), 44-45.

Dewey, J. (1933). *Experience and education.* New York: Macmillan.

Dewey, J. (1938). *How we think.* New York: Heath.

DiBella, A. J., & Nevis, E. C. (1998). *How organizations learn.* San Francisco: Jossey-Bass.

Dixon, N. (1994). *The organizational learning cycle: How we can learn collectively.* London: McGraw-Hill.

Dixon, N. M. (1992). Organizational learning: A review of the literature with implications for HRD professionals. *Human Resource Development Quarterly, 3*(1), 29-49.

Driscoll, M., & Preskill, H. (1996). The journey toward becoming a learning organization: Are we almost there? In K. E. Watkins & V. J. Marsick (Eds.), *Creating the learning organization* (Vol. 1, pp. 67-80). Alexandria, VA: American Society for Training and Development.

Drucker, P. F. (1997). The future that has already happened. *Harvard Business Review, 75*(5), 19-23.

Edwards, J. E., Thomas, M. D., Rosenfeld, P., & Booth-Kewley, S. (1996). *How to conduct organizational surveys.* Thousand Oaks, CA: Sage.

Fandt, P. M. (1991). The relationship of accountability and interdependent behavior to enhancing team consequences. *Group & Organization Studies, 16*(3), 300-312.

Fenman, Ltd. (1996, August). *Involving line managers in training and development.* (Available at www.fenman.co.uk/index.htm)

Fetterman, D. (1994). Empowerment evaluation. *Evaluation Practice, 15*(1), 1-15.

Fetterman, D. (1996). *Empowerment evaluation: Knowledge and tools for self-assessment and accountability.* Thousand Oaks, CA: Sage.

Fink, A. (1995). *How to design surveys.* Thousand Oaks, CA: Sage.

Fiol, C. M., & Lyles, M. A. (1985). Organizational learning. *Academy of Management Review, 10*, 803-813.

Fitz-Gibbon, C. T., & Morris, L. L. (1987). *How to analyze data.* Newbury Park, CA: Sage.

Fowler, F. J. (1993). *Survey research methods.* Thousand Oaks, CA: Sage.

Frame, J. D. (1995). *Managing projects in organizations.* San Francisco: Jossey-Bass.

Frey, J. H., & Oishi, S. M. (1995). *How to conduct interviews by telephone and in person.* Thousand Oaks, CA: Sage.

Friere, P. (1970). *Pedagogy of the oppressed.* New York: Seabury.

Fullan, M. (1993). *Change forces: Probing the depths of educational reform.* London: Falmer.

Galagan, P., & Wulf, K. (1996). Signs of the times. *Training & Development, 50*(2), 32-36.

Gardner, H. (1983). *Frames of mind.* New York: Basic Books.

Garvin, D. A. (1984, July 25). Asking questions is the key skill needed for "discussion teaching." *Chronicle of Higher Education,* p. 20.

Garvin, D. A. (1993). Building a learning organization. *Harvard Business Review, 71*(4), 78-91.

Gephart, M. A., Marsick, V. J., Van Buren, M. E., and Spiro, M. S. (1996). Learning organizations come alive. *Training & Development, 50*(12), 35-45.

Goddard, R. W. (1990). The rise of the new organization. *MW, 19*(1), 3-5.

Goodman, P., Sproull, L., & Associates. (1990). *Technology and organizations.* San Francisco: Jossey-Bass.

Graham, R. J., & Englund, R. L. (1997). *Creating an environment for successful projects.* San Francisco: Jossey-Bass.

Greenbaum, T. L. (1997). *The handbook for focus group research.* Thousand Oaks, CA: Sage.

Greene, J. C. (1988). Stakeholder participation and utilization in program evaluation. *Evaluation Review, 18*(5), 574-591.

Greene, J. C., & Caracelli, V. J. (Eds.). (1997). Advances in mixed-method evaluation: The challenges and benefits of integrating diverse paradigms [Special issue]. *New Directions for Evaluation, 74.*

Greer, M. (1996). *The project manager's partner.* Amherst, MA: Human Resource Development Press.

Guzzo, R. A., & Dickson, M. W. (1996). Teams in organizations: Recent research on performance and effectiveness. *Annual Review of Psychology, 47*, 307-338.

Hamilton-KSA Analysts. (1996). Demand for value in health care, part 3. *Perspectives.* Atlanta, GA: Author.

Harrington-Mackin, D. (1994). *The team building tool kit.* New York: American Management Association.

Harris, D. M., & DeSimone, R. L. (1994). *Human resource development.* Fort Worth, TX: The Dreydon Press, Harcourt Brace College Publishers.

Hastings, C. (1996). *The new organization.* London: McGraw-Hill.

Helgeson, S. (1995). *The web of inclusion: A new architecture for building great organizations.* New York: Currency/Doubleday.

Herman, J. L. (Ed.). (1987). *Program evaluation kit* (2nd ed.). Thousand Oaks, CA: Sage.

Hoffman, F., & Withers, B. (1995). Shared values: Nutrients for learning. In S. Chawla & J. Renesch (Eds.), *Learning organizations: Developing cultures for tomorrow's workplace* (pp. 463-474). Portland, OR: Productivity Press.

Hord, S. M. (1997). Professional learning communities: Communities of continuous inquiry and improvement. Austin, TX: Southwest Educational Development Laboratory.

Horvath, L., Callahan, J. L., Croswell, C., & Mukri, G. (1996, March). Team sensemaking: An imperative for individual and organizational learning. In E. F. Holton III (Ed.), *Academy of Human Resource Development Conference Proceedings*. Baton Rouge, LA: Academy of Human Resource Development.

Huber, G. P. (1991). Organizational learning: The contributing processes and the literatures. *Organizational Science 2*(1), 88-115.

Inchausti, R. (1993). *Spitwad sutras: Classroom teaching as sublime vocation.* Westport, CT: Bergin and Garvey.

Jackson, L., & MacIssac, D. (1994). Introducing a new approach to experiential learning. In L. Jackson & R. S. Caffarella (Eds.), *New directions for adult and continuing education, 55,* 17-27.

Jarvis, P. (1992). *Paradoxes of learning.* San Francisco: Jossey-Bass.

Jenlink, P. M., & Torres, R. T. (1995). The role of evaluation in schools as learning organizations. In P. M. Jenlink (Ed.), *Systemic change: Touchstones for future schools.* Palatine, IL: IRI/Skylight Training and Publishing.

Johnson, P. (1996). Population aging and employment policies. In R. Paton, G. Clark, G. Jones, J. Lewis, & P. Quintas (Eds.), *The new management reader* (pp. 4-12). London: Routledge.

Joint Committee on Standards for Educational Evaluation. (1994). *The personnel evaluation standards.* Newbury Park, CA: Sage.

Judy, R. W., & D'Amico, C. (1997). *Workforce 2020: Work and workers in the 21st century.* Indianapolis: Hudson Institute.

Kaner, S. (1996). *Facilitator's guide to participatory decision-making.* Gabriola Island, British Columbia, Canada: New Society Publishers.

Kemmis, S., & McTaggart, R. (1982). *The action research planner.* Geelong, Australia: Deakin University Press.

King, P. M., & Kitchener, K. S. (1994). *Developing reflective judgment.* San Francisco: Jossey-Bass.

Knowles, M. S. (1980). *The modern practice of adult education: From pedagogy to andragogy* (2nd ed.). New York: Cambridge Books.

Kofman, F., & Senge, P. (1993). Communities of commitment: The heart of learning organizations. *Organizational Dynamics, 22*(2), 5-23.

Kolb, D. (1984). *Experiential learning: Experience as the source of learning and development.* Englewood Cliffs, NJ: Prentice Hall.

Kotter, J. P. (1996). *Leading change.* Boston, MA: Harvard Business School Press.

Kvale, S. (1996). *Interviews: An introduction to qualitative research interviewing.* Thousand Oaks, CA: Sage.

Lave, J., & Wenger, E. (1991). *Situated learning: Legitimate peripheral participation.* New York: Cambridge University Press.

Leitch, C., Harrison, R., & Burgoyne, J. (1996, September). *Understanding the learning company: A constructivist approach.* Paper presented at the Organizational Learning and the Learning Organization Research Symposium, Lancaster University, Lancaster, UK.

Loveman, G. W., & Gabarro, J. J. (1991). The managerial implications of changing work force demographics: A scoping study. *Human Resource Management, 30*(1), 7-29.

Mandl, A., & Sethi, D. (1996). Either.or yields the theory of both. In F. Hesselbein, M. Goldsmith, & R. Beckhard (Eds.), *The leader of the future.* San Francisco: Jossey-Bass.

March, J. G. (1995). The future, disposable organizations and the rigidities of imagination. *Organization, 2*(3/4), 427-440.

Marquardt, M. (1996a). *Building the learning organization.* New York: Mc-Graw Hill.

Marquardt, M. J. (1996b). Cyberlearning: New possibilities for HRD. *Training & Development, 50*(11), 56-57.

Marquardt, M., & Reynolds, A. (1994). *The global learning organization.* Burr Ridge, IL: Irwin.

Marshall, C., & Rossman, G. B. (1994). *Designing qualitative research* (2nd ed.). Thousand Oaks, CA: Sage.

Marsick, V. J., & Neaman, P. G. (1996). Individuals who learn create organizations that learn. *New Directions for Adult and Continuing Education, 72*(Winter), 97-104.

Martinez, M. (1997). Work-life programs reap benefits. *HR Magazine, 42*(6), 110-114.

McGill, I., & Beaty, L. (1995). *Action learning: A guide for professional, management and educational development.* London: Kogan Page.

McGill, M. E., & Slocum, J. W. (1993). Unlearning the organization. *Organizational Dynamics, 22*(2), 67-79.

McKenney, J., Copeland, D., & Mason, R. (1995). *Waves of change.* Boston, MA: Harvard Business School Press.

McLagan, P., & Nel, C. (1995). *The age of participation.* San Francisco: Berrett-Koehler.

McLagan, P., & Nel, C. (1996). The shift to participation. *Perspectives on Business and Global Change, 10*(1), 47-59.

McTaggart, R. (1991). *Action research: A short modern history.* Geelong, Australia: Deakin University Press.

Merriam, S. B., & Caffarella, R. S. (1991). *Learning in adulthood.* San Francisco: Jossey-Bass.

Mertens, D. M. (1997). *Research methods in education and psychology: Integrating diversity with quantitative & qualitative approaches.* Thousand Oaks, CA: Sage.

Mezirow, J. (1991). *Transformative dimensions of adult learning.* San Francisco: Jossey-Bass.

Miles, M. B., & Huberman, A. M. (1994). *Qualitative data analysis: An expanded sourcebook* (2nd ed.). Thousand Oaks, CA: Sage.

Mink, O. G., Mink, B. P., Downes, E. A., & Owen, E. O. (1994). *Open organizations: A model for effectiveness, renewal, and intelligent change.* San Francisco: Jossey-Bass.

Mohrman, S. A., Cohen, S. G., & Mohrman, A. M. (1995). *Designing team-based organizations.* San Francisco: Jossey-Bass.

Moingeon, B., & Edmondson, A. (Eds.). (1996). *Organizational learning and competitive advantage.* London: Sage.

Morgan, D. L., & Krueger, R. A. (1997). *The focus group kit.* Thousand Oaks, CA: Sage.

Morris, L. E. (1995). Development strategies for the knowledge era. In S. Chawla & J. Renesch (Eds.), *Learning organizations: Developing cultures for tomorrow's workplace* (pp. 322-335). Portland, OR: Productivity Press.

Morris, L. L., Fitz-Gibbon, C. T., & Freeman, M. E. (1987). *How to communicate evaluation findings.* Newbury Park, CA: Sage.

Morse, J. M. (1997). *Completing a qualitative project: Details and dialogue.* Thousand Oaks, CA: Sage.

Myers, I. B., & McCaulley, M. H. (1985). *Manual: A guide to the development and use of the Myers-Briggs Type Indicator.* Palo Alto, CA: Consulting Psychologists Press.

Neck, C. P., & Manz, C. C. (1994). From groupthink to teamthink: Toward the creation of constructive thought patterns in self-managing work teams. *Human Relations, 47*(8), 929-949.

Newcomer, K. E. (1997). Using performance measurement to improve programs. In K. E. Newcomer (Ed.), *Using performance measurement to improve public and nonprofit programs* (New Directions for Evaluation No. 75). San Francisco: Jossey-Bass.

Nonaka, I., & Takeuchi, H. (1995). *The knowledge-creating company.* New York: Oxford University Press.

Owen, H. (1992). *Open space technology: A user's guide.* Potomac, MD: Abbott.

Palmer, P. (1987). Community, conflict, and ways of knowing. *Change, 19*(5), 20-25.

Patton, M. Q. (1994). Developmental evaluation. *Evaluation Practice, 15*(3), 311-319.

Patton, M. Q. (1997). *Utilization-focused evaluation: The new century text* (3rd ed.). Thousand Oaks, CA: Sage.

Payne, D. A. (1994). *Designing educational project and program evaluations: A practical overview based on research and experience.* Boston: Kluwer.

Peck, M. S. (1987). *The different drum.* New York: Simon & Schuster.

Percival, A. (1996). Invited reaction: An adult educator responds. *Human Resource Development Quarterly, 7*(2), 131-139.

Peters, T. (1992). *Liberation management.* New York: Knopf.

Peterson, D. B., & Hicks, M. D. (1997). How to. *Training & Development, 51*(3), 9.

Phillips, R. I., & Phillips, A. (1995). Cognitive distortions: Barriers to change. *TQM Network News* (Spring). Alexandria, VA: American Society for Training and Development.

Posavac, E. J., & Carey, R. G. (1997). *Program evaluation methods and case studies* (5th ed.). Upper Saddle River, NJ: Prentice Hall.

Postman, N., & Weingartner, C. (1969). *Teaching as a subversive activity.* New York: Delacorte.

Preskill, H. (1991, October). *Metaphors of educational reform implementation: A case study of the Saturn School of Tomorrow.* Paper presented at the annual meeting of the American Evaluation Association, Chicago, IL.

Preskill, H. (1994). Evaluation's role in enhancing organizational learning: A model for practice. *Evaluation and Program Planning, 17*(3), 291-297.

Preskill, H. (1997, March). *HRD evaluation as the catalyst for organizational learning.* Paper presented at the annual meeting of the Academy of Human Resource Development, Atlanta, GA.

Preskill, H., Lackey, R., & Caracelli, V. (1997, November). *Expanding theoretical conceptions of evaluation misuse: Lessons from practice.* Paper presented at the annual meeting of the American Evaluation Association, San Diego, CA.

Preskill, S., & Preskill, H. (1997). Meeting the postmodern challenge: Pragmatism and evaluative inquiry for organizational learning. *Advances in Program Evaluation, 3,* 155-169.

Revans, R. (1982). *The origin and growth of action learning.* Bickly, Kent, UK: Chartwell-Bratt.

Rogers, C. R. (1969). *Freedom to learn.* Columbus, OH: Merrill.

Rubin, H. J., & Rubin, I. S. (1995). *Qualitative interviewing: The art of hearing data.* Thousand Oaks, CA: Sage.

Ryan, S. (1995). Learning communities: An alternative to the expert model. In S. Chawla & J. Renesch (Eds.), *Learning organizations: Developing cultures for tomorrow's workplace* (pp. 279-291). Portland, OR: Productivity Press.

Saban, J. M., Killion, J. P., & Green, C. G. (1994). The centric reflection model: A kaleidoscope for staff developers. *Journal of Staff Development, 15*(3), 16-20.

Sapsford, R., & Jupp, V. (Eds.). (1996). *Data collection and analysis.* Thousand Oaks, CA: Sage.

Schein, E. H. (1996). The cultures of management: The key to organizational learning. *Sloan Management Review, 38*(1), 9-20.

Schon, D. A. (1983). *The reflective practitioner.* New York: Basic Books.

Schon, D. A. (1987). *Educating the reflective practitioner.* San Francisco: Jossey-Bass.

Schrage, M. (1989). *No more teams!: Mastering the dynamics of creative collaboration.* New York: Currency.

Schratz, M. (1993). From cooperative action to collective self-reflection: A sociodynamic approach to educational research. In M. Schratz (Ed.), *Qualitative voices in educational research* (Social Research and Educational Series No. 10). London: Falmer.

Schwandt, D. R. (1995). Learning as an organization: A journey into chaos. In S. Chawla & J. Renesch (Eds.), *Learning organizations: Developing cultures for tomorrow's workplace* (pp. 365-380). Portland, OR: Productivity Press.

Schwandt, T. A. (1992). Better living through evaluation? Images of progress shaping evaluation practice. *Evaluation Practice, 13*(2), 135-144.

Schwandt, T. A. (1997). Evaluation as practical hermeneutics. *Evaluation, 3*(1), 69-83.

Schwarz, R. M. (1994). Ground rules for groups. *Training & Development, 48*(8), 45-53.

Senge, P. M. (1990a). *The fifth discipline.* New York: Doubleday.

Senge, P. M. (1990b). The leaders' new work: Building learning organizations. *Sloan Management Review, 32*(1), 19-35.

Senge, P. M. (1996). Leading learning organizations: The bold, the powerful, and the invisible. In F. Hesselbein, M. Goldsmith, & R. Beckhard (Eds.), *The leader of the future* (pp. 41-57). San Francisco: Jossey-Bass.

Senge, P. M., Roberts, C., Ross, R. B., Smith, B. J., & Kleiner, A. (1994). *The fifth discipline fieldbook.* New York: Doubleday.

Sergiovanni, T. J. (1994). *Building community in schools.* San Francisco: Jossey-Bass.

Shadish, W. R., Jr., Cook, T. D., & Leviton, L. C. (1991). *Foundations of program evaluation: Theories and practice.* Newbury Park, CA: Sage.

Shapiro, J. P. (1988). Participatory evaluation: Towards a transformation of assessment for women's studies programs and projects. *Educational Evaluation and Policy Analysis, 11*(5), 555-590.

Shaw, R. B., & Perkins, D.N.T. (1991). Teaching organizations to learn. *Organization Development Journal, 9*(4), 1-12.

Sheley, E. (1996). Share your worth. *HR Magazine, 41*(6), 86.

Sirkin, R. M. (1994). *Statistics for the social sciences.* Thousand Oaks, CA: Sage.

Spear, S. (1993). The emergence of learning communities. *The systems thinker.* Cambridge, MA: Pegasus Communications.

Stake, R. E. (1995). *The art of case study research.* Thousand Oaks, CA: Sage.

Stamps, D. (1997). Communities of practice. *Training, 34*(2), 34-42.

Stecher, B. M., & Davis, W. A. (1987). *How to focus an evaluation.* Thousand Oaks, CA: Sage.

Stewart, T. A. (1997). *Intellectual capital.* New York: NY: Doubleday/Currency.

Tapscott, D. (1995). *The digital economy.* New York: Basic Books.

Thompson, J. W. (1995). The renaissance of learning in business. In S. Chawla & J. Renesch (Eds.), *Learning organizations: Developing cultures for tomorrow's workplace* (pp. 85-99). Portland, OR: Productivity Press.

Torres, R. T. (1991). Improving the quality of internal evaluation: The evaluator as consultant-mediator. *Evaluation and Program Planning, 14*(3) 189-198.

Torres, R. T., Preskill, H. S., & Piontek, M. E. (1996). *Evaluation strategies for communicating and reporting: Enhancing learning in organizations.* Thousand Oaks, CA: Sage.

Torres, R. T., Preskill, H., & Piontek, M. (1997). Communicating and reporting: Concerns of internal and external evaluators. *Evaluation Practice, 18*(2), 105-125.

Tough, A. (1979). *The adult's learning projects: A fresh approach to theory and practice in adult learning* (2nd ed.). Toronto: Ontario Institute for Studies in Education.

Training Magazine Industry Report. (1994, October). *Training Magazine, 31*(10), 59-66.

Training Magazine Industry Report. (1997, October). *Training Magazine, 34*(10), 35-75.

Trist, E. L. (1981, June). *The evolution of socio-technical systems: A conceptual framework and an action research program* (Occasional Paper No. 2). Toronto: Ontario Quality of Working Life Centre.

Vaill, P. (1996). *Learning as a way of being.* San Francisco: Jossey-Bass.

Van de Ven, A. H., & Grazman, D. N. (1995). *Technological innovation, learning, and leadership.* Paper presented at the Stern School of Business Research of New York University, New York.

Watkins, K. E. (1996). Of course organizations learn! *New Directions for Adult and Continuing Education, 72*(Winter), 89-94.

Watkins, K. E., & Marsick, V. J. (1992). Building the learning organization: A new role for human resource developers. *Studies in Continuing Education, 14*(2), 115-129.

Watkins, K. E., & Marsick, V. J. (1993). *Sculpting the learning organization.* San Francisco: Jossey-Bass.

Watkins, K. E., & Marsick, V. J. (Eds.). (1996). *Creating the learning organization* (Vol. 1). Alexandria, VA: American Society for Training and Development.

Weeks, D. (1992). *Conflict resolution.* New York: G. P. Putnam's Sons.

Weisbord, M. R. (1987). *Productive workplaces.* San Francisco: Jossey-Bass.

Wenger, E. (1997). Practice, learning, meaning, identity. *Training, 34*(2), 38-39.

Wheatley, M. J. (1994). Leadership and the new science. San Francisco: Berrett-Koehler.

Wick, C. W., & Leon, L. S. (1993). *The learning edge.* New York: McGraw-Hill.

Willis, V., & May, G. (1997). The chief learning officer: A case study at Millbrook Distribution Services. In H. Preskill & R. Dilworth (Eds.), *HRD in transition: Defining the cutting edge.* Washington, DC: International Society for Performance Improvement.

Wolcott, H. F. (1994). *Transforming qualitative data: Description, analysis, and interpretation.* Thousand Oaks, CA: Sage.

Worthen, B. R., Sanders, J. R., & Fitzpatrick, J. L. (1997). *Program evaluation: Alternative approaches and practical guidelines* (2nd ed.). New York: Longman.

Wright, D. B. (1996). *Understanding statistics: An introduction for the social sciences.* Thousand Oaks, CA: Sage.

Wysocki, R. K., Beck, R., & Crane, D. B. (1995). *Effective project management: How to plan, manage, and deliver projects on time and within budget.* New York: John Wiley & Sons.

Young, D. P., & Dixon, N. M. (1996). *Helping leaders take effective action: A program evaluation.* Greensboro, NC: Center for Creative Leadership.

Zand, D. E. (1997). *The leadership triad: Knowledge, trust, and power.* New York: Oxford University Press.

Zuboff, S. (1988). *In the age of the smart machine.* New York: Basic Books.

Index

About the Authors

Hallie Preskill, PhD, is an Associate Professor and Program Coordinator/Graduate Advisor in the Organizational Learning and Instructional Technologies graduate program at the University of New Mexico, Albuquerque. She teaches introductory and advanced courses in program evaluation, organizational learning, and instructional design. Prior to her current position, she was a faculty member at the University of St. Thomas in Minneapolis/St. Paul, Minnesota, for 7 years; was the Training Director for Plato/Wicat Systems; and was an external training consultant for Control Data. Her research interests focus on program evaluation theory, methods, and use; organizational learning; and the transfer of learning. She is coauthor of the book *Evaluation Strategies for Communicating and Reporting: Enhancing Learning in Organizations* (Torres, Preskill, & Piontek, 1996) and coeditor of *Human Resource Development Review* (Russ-Eft, Preskill, & Sleezer, 1997). Over the past 18 years, she has written numerous articles and book chapters on evaluation methods and processes and on the role of evaluation in training and development. During these years, she also conducted more than 20 program evaluations and provided evaluation and instructional design consulting services to business, education, nonprofit, and human services organizations. She received her PhD in Program Evaluation and Training and Development from the University of Illinois at Urbana-Champaign in 1984.

Rosalie T. Torres, PhD, is Director of Research at Developmental Studies Center (DSC), a nonprofit educational organization in Oakland, California, that develops programs and materials to help elementary schools strengthen children's social, ethical, and intellectual development. Dr. Torres is responsible for implementing a participatory, organizational learning approach to the evaluation of DSC's programs. Previously, she ran her own research and management consulting firm specializing in the feedback-based development of individuals, teams, and organizations. She also was an Assistant Professor at Western Michigan University, where she taught courses in program and personnel evaluation as well as working on the development of program evaluation standards for the Joint Committee on Standards for Educational Evaluation. She earned her PhD in research and evaluation in 1989 from the University of Illinois at Urbana-Champaign. Over the past 20 years, she has conducted more than 40 evaluations in education, business, health care, and nonprofit organizations. She has worked as an internal evaluator for the Dallas Independent School District, the Chicago Public Schools, and the Colorado Springs School District. Dr. Torres is coauthor of a previous book addressing the role of evaluation in organizational learning, *Evaluation Strategies for Communicating and Reporting: Enhancing Learning in Organizations* (1996). She presents at evaluation conferences annually and has published several articles on the practice of evaluation.